Walking the Ulster Way

A Journal and a Guide

Alan Warner

Maps drawn
by Kilian McDaid

Appletree Press

to Hazel
who helped and supported me
in so many ways

Published and printed by
The Appletree Press
7 James Street South
Belfast BT2 8DL.

Second edition 1989
Copyright © Alan Warner, 1983, 1989
Maps copyright © Kilian McDaid,
1983, 1989

British Library Cataloguing
in Publication Data
Warner, Alan, 1912 -
    Walking the Ulster way: a journal and
    a guide.
    1. Northern Ireland. Long distance
    footpaths: Ulster way. Description &
    travel
    1. Title H. Warner, Alan 1912-. On foot
    in Ulster 914.16'04824

    ISBN 0-86281-227-5

9 8 7 6 5 4 3 2 1

Contents

Acknowledgments

My grateful thanks are due to the Dean of The School of Biological and Environmental Sciences at the New University of Ulster, Dr K. I. Wallwork, and to the Geography department of this School for assistance with the maps in this book. In particular I wish to thank Shirley Tinkler and Kilian McDaid for their cheerful, willing and efficient help. I also received much help and advice from the Sports Council for Northern Ireland, in particular from Wilfred Capper and Danny O'Connor. The Northern Ireland Tourist Board kindly provided photographs for Part One and Bord Failte did the same for Part Two. Nigel Jess, who knows much about rural Ulster assisted me in many ways. In planning and walking the routes in Donegal, I had much help from Gaye Moynihan, formerly of the Planning Department, Donegal County Council, who was a keen promoter of Sli Ulaidh. Finally I acknowledge the friendly encouragement that I received at all times from other walkers, from Wilfred Capper himself, 'the father of the Ulster Way', and from Dick Rogers, who accompanied and guided me on Day 23, and from all my friends in the Bannside Ramblers whose interest and support was unfailing.

Abbreviation: The initials S.C. in the marginal notes stand for the Sports Council of Northern Ireland.

Preface

This book consists of two parts. The first originally appeared in 1983 under the title *On Foot in Ulster*. This mainly consists of a journal giving a day by day account of a long walk undertaken by the author in the spring of 1979, when he followed the Ulster Way round the whole province of Northern Ireland. One or two marginal notes have been added to bring information up to date, but the text of the original journal remains unchanged.

The second part of this book contains new material, dealing with the extension of the Ulster Way in Co. Donegal, and with some other walking routes in this county. The walks were undertaken between 1982 and 1987.

Keys to the Maps

Each part of the book has its own separate key to the maps, because the maps in Part Two are drawn in a somewhat different style from those in Part One, and they incorporate the change to the metric system that has been made in Co. Donegal.

Part One
The Ulster Way

A Song of the Ulster Way

I took a walk in Ulster,
The Way is long to tell,
I went by Fairy water
And over Bessy Bell.

By Little Dog and Big Dog,
Lough Formal and Lough Doo,
I followed on the Lakeland Way
Until I reached Belcoo.

I passed the lonely crossroads
At Eshywulligan,
I stopped at Keady Orlit
And Lough na Blaney Bane.

Past Ballygawley Water
I walked to Aughnacloy,
I went by Legatillida,
By Maghery and Moy.

By Ramaket and Ballynure
Drumgruff and Quiggy Hill,
By Pettigoe and Swanlinbar,
Drumlee and Columbcille,

Fardross and Favor Royal,
Moydamlaght and Glenshane,
Benburb and Ballycullen,
Bannfoot and Crabtreelane.

All these were on the way I went,
Their names spelt out my track,
And still their echo haunts my mind
As I lay down my pack.

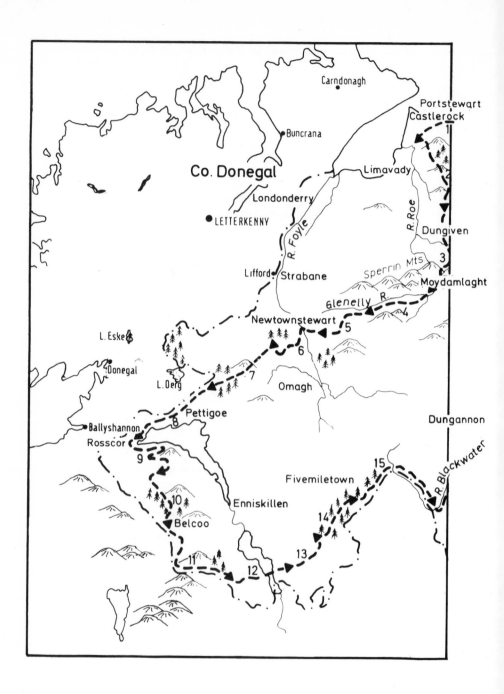

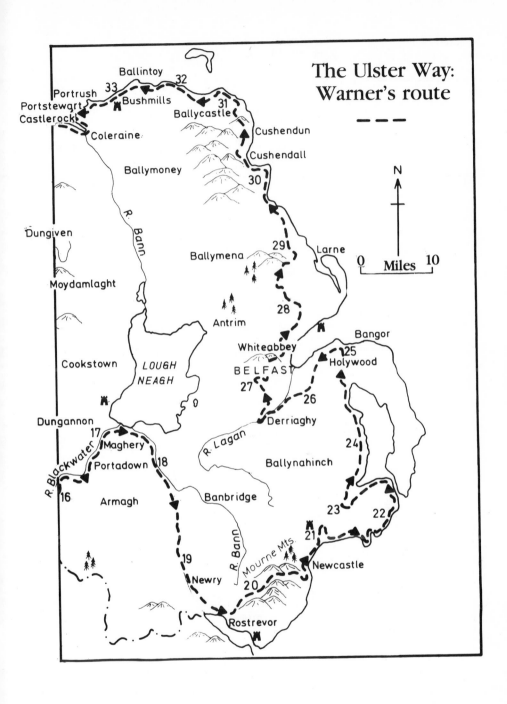

The Ulster Way: Warner's route

- - - -

N

0   Miles   10

Key to Maps (Part One)

▶	Start Of Day's Walk
■	Finish Of Day's Walk
— — —	Warner's Route
XXXXXXXXX	Sports Council Route
• • • • • • • • • • •	Low Level Route
— — — —	Hiker's Trail
Mourne Wall	Mourne Wall
— · — · —	Border
	Road
M.1	Motorway
Dual Carriageway	Dual Carriageway
—+—+—+—	Railway Line
R. Bann	River
	Lake And Sea
1000'	Contours Shown In Feet
	Wooded Area
	Large Area Of Population
▲ Y.H.	Youth Hostel
• 1221	Spot Height (Feet)
⊐⊏	Bridge
ᵛ ↓ ᵛ	Marsh
	Cliff

Introduction

The images of Ulster that have dominated the news media for the past ten years have been urban and violent, yet most of Ulster is pastoral and peaceful. There is only one city of any real size, namely Belfast, and even here from most of the city's streets you can lift your eyes towards a vista of green hills. To the walker Ulster offers a great deal of unspoilt country-side of real beauty and great variety, and it has a magnificent long-distance route—the Ulster Way.

'Ulster' was originally a geographical area, the most northerly of the four provinces of Ireland, the other three being Leinster, Munster and Connaught, but the name is commonly used today to indicate the relatively new state of Northern Ireland, established after the partition of Ireland in 1921. The Ulster Way keeps for the most part within the boundary of Northern Ireland, only briefly and occasionally overlapping into the old Ulster in the counties of Donegal and Cavan. It should be noted, however, that the Donegal County Council are currently planning and preparing a large extension of the route to make a circuit of Donegal, all of which is excellent walking country. This extension links up with the Ulster Way at Pettigoe, a small town on the border of Fermanagh and Donegal, close to Lower Lough Erne.

Such a circuit now seems unlikely. See Part Two for more information about Donegal.

The Ulster Way itself makes a complete circuit of Ulster, passing through much varied and beautiful scenery. It strikes north from Belfast over the Antrim hills, then sweeps round the North Coast, a dramatic coastline with rocky headlands, high cliffs and curving sandy bays. From Castlerock, at the mouth of the Foyle estuary, it swings south through forest tracks and over hills into the Sperrin mountains. Thence it moves south–west to Lough Erne, and through the lakes and gentle hills of Fermanagh to the remote Cuilcagh mountain range on the border with Cavan.

13

It follows roughly the irregular line of the border, and then goes north–east down the Blackwater river to Lough Neagh, moving south again through Portadown on the Bann, and along the old Newry canal towards the Mourne mountains. It crosses the Mournes to Newcastle and then heads north up the coast towards Belfast to complete the circle. The total distance is about 500 miles.

The Ulster Way is not yet completed. Only about a quarter of the trail is waymarked and provided with stiles. Some parts of the route follow existing roads and lanes, but in other parts the walker must strike out over open moorland and mountain, with little to guide him except map and compass. But the work of waymarking and plotting the route is steadily proceeding under the expert guidance of Wilfrid Capper, who is currently acting as footpaths officer for the Sports Council of Northern Ireland. Wilfrid Capper is indeed the father of the Ulster Way. Its conception and development has been very largely due to his enthusiasm and persistence. Long ago, in 1946, he walked the Pennine Way with Tom Stephenson, and when he returned to Ireland he was determined that Ulster should have a Way of its own. His dream has now become a reality. The Way is there, waiting for the feet of walkers.

It turned out that I was the first person to walk right round the Ulster Way, with one or two very small omissions, which will be explained in my journal. I happened to hear of the Way at a time when I was soon to retire from my post as Professor of English at the New University of Ulster in Coleraine. I had always been fond of walking, and for a long time I had cherished the hope of doing a long-distance walk. Retirement gave me the leisure to plan and carry it out. I had thought about the Pennine Way and the South West coastal path through Dorset, Devon and Cornwall; but when I heard of the Ulster Way, and that no one had yet been round it, it seemed the obvious route for me to choose. It was almost on my

Now, in 1989, the route is much more developed, and the bulk of it is waymarked.

doorstep, since I lived in Coleraine; it offered a very substantial long-distance walk, and it presented an exciting challenge.

My first problem was to get an adequate idea of the route to be followed, by no means a simple proposition. It was less a matter of following a route than of blazing a trail. In the spring of 1979, the time I chose to make my pilgrimage, less than fifty miles of the route had been waymarked, and nearly half of this was on a loop line (the Moyle Way from Ballycastle to Glenariff) which was not part of the main route. I soon got in touch with Wilfrid Capper and I had long sessions with him poring over the one-inch Ordnance Survey maps for Ulster, all nine of them. Without his patient help I could never have made a start on my journey.

Anyone who has tried to follow an unmarked route through unfamiliar country by studying a map will realise that map work alone is not enough. It is necessary to get a look at the ground too. No map is ever completely up to date, and quite apart from this, a feature which is prominent on the map, such as a lake or even a mountain, turns out to be invisible when you are on the ground at a particular point in a particular kind of weather. So I spent a considerable time making reconnoitring expeditions to explore the ground in what seemed to me the more difficult and unfamiliar parts of the route.

I combined my preliminary route-finding with an attempt to find accommodation for the nights I intended to spend on the Way. At the beginning I had decided that, at the age of 66, I was too old and not tough enough to carry a heavy load, including a tent and provisions, that would enable me to camp at night. So I planned to reach the shelter of a house every evening to find a meal and a bed. Although I studied all the available literature on places to stay in Northern Ireland, I soon discovered that there were many parts of the route where it was quite impossible to find any kind of public overnight accommodation. So I had to knock on private doors, explain my situation and ask if there was any house in the neighbourhood where I might find a bed for the night. Sometimes I was lucky. At Keady Orlit in Fermanagh, near Lisnaskea, the first door I tried brought a friendly and hospitable welcome. Mrs McAdam at once offered me a bed when I should require it. In other places I had a long and tedious search before I found someone willing to take me in.

At Caledon I was nearly in despair, after I had tried several places in vain; but I ended up with a bed in Caledon Castle, a truly magnificent bed as it turned out, a Georgian four-poster in white and gold. I wrote to Lord Caledon explaining my predicament and asking him if there was anyone on his estate who might give me a night's lodging. He and Lady Caledon very kindly offered me the hospitality of their own home. So my overnight accommodation ranged from high to low, from Caledon Castle to a seedy little guest-house, not listed in any tourist guide, where I had a sagging bed with a naked light bulb overhead. In general I was lodged with great comfort, and fed like a prince. In all the private houses where I stayed I was received with genuine warmth, and not one of the good samaritans who fed and sheltered me would take any reward. Throughout my reconnoitring expeditions, and on the walk itself, I met with friendliness and kindness of all kinds. For example, on the Fermanagh–Cavan border I asked the first man I saw if he could tell me where I might try to find accommodation. He not only told me where to try, but he lent me his bicycle to ride there and back, to save me time, since it was not possible to cross the border by car at this point. I was a complete stranger, and might have ridden away on his bicycle, but in rural Ulster such suspicions are not harboured.

Not all my time was spent on the search for accommodation. Much of it was devoted to route-finding, and I learnt one or two salutary lessons about Ulster hills and forests. On one occasion I was overtaken by darkness in the Mournes and more or less lost. My wife, whom I had arranged to meet at a point on the Kilkeel–Hilltown road, went to Kilkeel police station to report my absence. Once again I was helped by a good samaritan, a friendly farmer on a remote hill farm near Attical. This misadventure, which might have been more unpleasant than it finally turned out, was due to my starting on a reconnoitring walk much too late on an autumn day. I wanted to explore a part of the route from Rostrevor to Newcastle, since the country was quite strange to me. (This was in 1978, before the publication of the excellent Outdoor Pursuits map of the Mourne Country (scale 1:25,000) which clearly marks in the Ulster Way.) My wife dropped me in Rostrevor Forest, and I was to meet her on the road some two hours later. After about an hour and a half, I realised that I had grossly underestimated the time needed to reach the road. Darkness was falling, the going was very rough and I had no light except for a small pocket torch with a nearly flat battery. I decided to abandon any attempt to reach the road at the point agreed on, and to try to get off the hills by following a stream down a valley leading south. Even this proved to be difficult, but at length I saw a dim light in what looked like a group of farm buildings. After crossing the stream and climbing a wall, I managed to grope my way to the door. I was brought in to a warm fire, where I explained what had happened. There was no telephone at the farm, but the farmer told me where I was, and where I would find the nearest telephone. Indeed, in spite of my protests, he insisted on coming with me to Attical, where he took me into a friend's house and found me a phone. I rang the police station at Kilkeel, and found that my wife was actually there, reporting my absence. So all ended well, thanks to the kindly farmer, who insisted on waiting with me until my wife arrived in the car to collect me. After this episode I was more careful not to let darkness overtake me in unfamiliar countryside.

I had decided to tackle the Ulster Way by myself, without seriously trying to find a companion, partly because I am naturally a loner, and partly because I had no enthusiastic walking friend who could give up a month of his time in the spring. Many people asked me if I wasn't worried about being alone on the hills in bad weather. What would I do if I fell and broke an ankle? This question is not easy to answer. I suppose I would crawl towards help as best I could. There is an element of risk in walking alone, but one cannot live satisfactorily without taking risks of some sort. It is risky to ride a bicycle, or even to drive a car. I am not defending foolhardiness, but the attempt to eliminate all risks finally becomes ridiculous. I remember hearing once of a fond mother who advised her offspring: 'Keep your mouths closed always for fear of taking in germs'.

I did take what precautions I could by letting my wife and the Sports Council have full details of where I would be each night, and I arranged that every evening I would telephone Sergeant Ken MacClean, a police liason officer with the Mountain Rescue Services, just to report that all was well. This arrangment proved reasonably satisfactory, but it was sometimes very difficult for me to find a telephone. Once, after what turned out to be my worst day, it was impossible, because I was staying in Swanlinbar, during a phone strike in the Republic of Ireland.

When I began to plan this walk it was purely a private whim, for my own pleasure and satisfaction, but as time went on I found that I had become deeply involved, first with the Sports Council, and then with the Northern Ireland Tourist Board. Both these bodies gave me help and encouragement, and I had promised to write reports for them both on different aspects of the Way. Then I was approached by the Samaritans in Coleraine, who asked if they could sponsor me to raise money for their organisation. I readily agreed to this, but it meant another commitment. Finally the BBC in Belfast got in touch with me to ask if I would ring them during my walk and report progress. I naturally agreed, and was rather flattered by the publicity I was getting.

I was now involved up to the neck, and I had not yet started on the walk. As the starting day grew nearer, I began to have misgivings. Had I bitten off more than I could chew? What a flop it would be if I had to retire halfway round the Ulster Way, or even earlier. But it was too late for second thoughts now. The route was planned, my accommodation was booked for every night, so I must set out and try to keep to my schedule. At least I was not trying to set up a speed record. I was aiming at a modest average of 15 miles a day, though there were some days when I would have to do 20 to reach my next night's lodging. I had 33 days to complete my 495 miles.

Finally I put aside my misgivings, packed my rucksack and set off from Portstewart Harbour at 9.30 am on March 28th, 1979. From this point I will let my diary tell the story of my long spring walk.

I started from Portstewart because it was near my home, and I chose to make the circuit anti-clockwise. This took me through the loneliest and most remote part of the country first, leaving me the more populated east and north coasts, where it was easier to find lodging at night, for the later part of my walk.

Day 1 Wednesday 28 March: Portstewart to Largantea

Before it runs into the sea near Castlerock the river Bann forms quite a wide estuary. Small ships sail up river to the harbour in Coleraine. The railway bridge, carrying the track to Londonderry, is a cantilever structure that opens to let them through.

The low-lying shores at the Barmouth are much frequented by water birds of all kinds, and there is a bird sanctuary on the west bank of the river, a few hundred yards above the small cluster of houses known as 'Barmouth'. There is a hide at the water's edge that offers an excellent viewing point for patient bird-watchers.

I had a good send-off to-day at Portstewart Harbour on a fine dry morning with a stiff north-westerly wind blowing. Several friends had gathered to wish me well, and a group of girls from the nearby Dominican Convent School had been brought by one of their teachers. Their bare knees looked chilly in the cold wind. Wilfrid Capper had come all the way from Holywood that morning, and he walked with me along the coast as far as the river Bann. I had already made a special arrangement to be ferried across the river near the mouth, thus avoiding a walk into Coleraine to cross the bridge, and out again to Castlerock. Ronnie McGeagh of the Coleraine Borough Council, which manages the local marina, brought out his rescue boat for me. The stiff wind made the river mouth rough and choppy, and we had some difficulty in crossing. We had to go upstream to the point where the Articlave River flows into the Bann. Ronnie managed to land me here, but he could not get the boat out again into deep water against the strong wind. After a few unsuccessful attempts, he decided that he would have to wait for the tide to fall, and I agreed to telephone the Borough Council as soon as I could and explain the position.

I crossed the Articlave river by the railway bridge and walked across the fields to the houses at the Bar mouth, and knocked on a likely door. This was the first of many doors that I was to knock on in the course of the next month, and at every one of them I was lucky enough to get a friendly reception. At this door I found a young mother with a toddler. She not only allowed me to use her telephone, but while I was doing so she made me a cup of coffee.

I walked on over the golf links to Castlerock and through the town to the cliff path past the caravan site. The cliff edge was exposed to the full force of

21

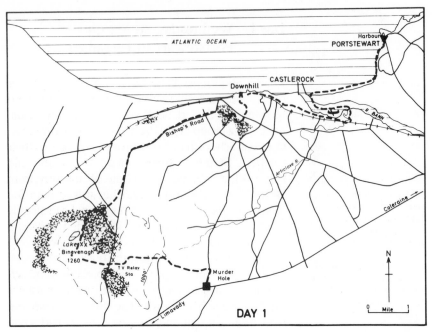

DAY 1

the wind which raged and screamed at me through the mesh wire fence. I went down into the Black Glen, past the north end of the Bishop's Fish Pond and found shelter behind the wall at the top of the steps, where I had lunch sitting in the sun.

The Downhill Demesne, now a National Trust property, once belonged to the rich and eccentric Lord Hervey, Earl–Bishop of Derry in the latter part of the eighteenth century. He built a magnificent castle-palace in the seventeen-seventies. This is now a roofless ruin, but it is still imposing, standing on high ground above the sea between Castlerock and Downhill. Even better known than the ruined castle is the fine temple, built right on the edge of a high cliff looking across the waters of Lough Foyle to the hills of Inishowen. It is indeed, in the words of the National Trust guide book, 'a unique and perfect blend of sophisticated elegance with natural un-adorned beauty'. The design is based on the classic Temples of Vesta at Tivoli and Rome. It was

The Ulster Way is now waymarked from Castlerock to near Dungiven and it is routed straight up the Black Glen to the Bishop's Gate. My own route followed the coastline westwards to pass the Mussenden Temple. I would recommend this short diversion to anyone following the waymarked route.

22

Mussenden Temple, over-looking the entrance to Lough Foyle

completed in 1785 and named after the Bishop's cousin, Mrs Mussenden.

From the temple I returned to the Glen and going out through the Bishop's Gate passed through Downhill Forest, up the side of an attractive little waterfall and so to the Bishop's road above Downhill. The route follows this road over the open hills towards Binevenagh. At first I had some shelter from the hedges, but higher up I was exposed to the full force of the wind again. I could hardly stand up in it when I turned aside at the Gortmore viewpoint to look out over the wide sweep of Magilligan below. Even my beard was plucked and shaken. I recalled some lines from Ted Hughes's poem 'Wind':

Magilligan Strand, which runs from Downhill to Magilligan Point, is Ireland's longest beach. It is a fine wide strand, much frequented by bass fishermen, and sometimes used for sand-yachting.

> Through the brunt wind that dented the balls of
> my eyes
> The tent of the hills drummed and strained its
> guy-rope,

23

The fields quivering, the skyline a grimace,
At any second to bang and vanish with a flap:
The wind flung a magpie away and a black-
back gull bent like an iron bar slowly. . .

Normally when I am walking I fall naturally into a train of thought, but when the wind is teasing and battering me I find that no such relaxing is possible. The rhythm of walking is shaken and interrupted.

Before long I was entering the welcome shelter of Binevenagh Forest and I worked my way up through the pine trees to the edge of the escarpment, and then I followed this to the lake near the summit of Binevenagh. I went on over the summit round the southern edge of the lake, and then I made a beeline across the bog for the TV mast, which marks the route through Grange Park. I followed the forest track through the Grange Park plantations until I reached the 'murder-hole' road. This was the end of my stint for the day. Because I was still near home I had arranged for my wife to pick me up, and then return me to this point next morning.

The old road from Coleraine to Limavady is still known as the Murderhole road. The name dates back to the eighteenth century, when some murderer, perhaps the notorious highwayman, Cushy Glen, threw his victims into a bog-hole.

Day 2   Thursday 29 March:
to Legavannon Pot

To-day my rucksack was noticeably heavier, because now I am staying each night on the route with no returns to base. My load only weighed about 25 lb., which is light by back-packing standards, but I found it heavy enough, especially during the last two hours of the walking day, and I was often looking for ways of lightening it, by sending things ahead of me when I could.

I was unlucky enough to develop a sore toe on my first day's walk. I think I must have bruised it some-how before the walk began. So I paid a quick visit to the Coleraine Health Centre before setting out, where I was relieved to learn that the toe was not infected. I had a light cottonwool dressing put on it, and I left with good hope that it would not be a serious handicap. It was my only physical handicap on the walk, but fortunately it never became really painful.

I started again from the 'Murder Hole' road and most of the day my way was on forest tracks. I turned south through Springwell Forest, crossed the main

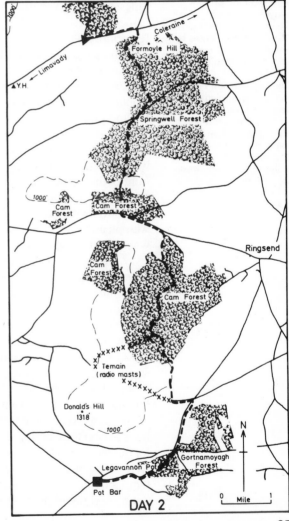

Coleraine–Limavady Road and continued south over the shoulder of Keady mountain, to the Limavady–Garvagh Road. After following this for half a mile I entered Cam Forest and continued moving south. I had lunch in a sheltered spot by a small dam. After lunch it began to snow, so I put on my waterproof anorak and overtrousers and battled on, passing out of the forest, over a stretch of bog and on to the Ringsend–Dungiven road, which runs through Gortnamoyagh Forest and round the edge of Legavannon Pot.

Turning right at the Pot Bridge I soon came to the Pot Bar, and since there are very few bars or pubs on the direct line of the Ulster Way, I decided that it would be a good idea to go in for a bottle of Guinness. But the place seemed deserted and the front doors were firmly shut. When I went round to the back, I discovered that there was a good reason for this—it was to keep out the strong cold wind blowing at the front of the house. The young woman in charge, Mrs Quigg, brought me into the bar the back way and served me with a bottle of Guinness which I drank with pleasure. I still had time in hand, since the farm where I was to spend the night was only half a mile away, and I was still thirsty; so I asked if it was possible to get a cup of tea. Mrs Quigg very obligingly made me tea, and brought me in to the turf fire in her sitting room. She also made me some sandwiches, and when I later proferred payment she would take no money.

As I was passing through the kitchen I noticed a small lamb in a polythene barrel. Apparently the mother had no milk for it, and it had been brought into the house to be fed with a bottle. I was told that the prolonged cold wintry weather had made it a very hard season for lambing. There was no spring grass for the mothers. While I was there some more lambs were brought in suffering from cold, and given a temporary home in the warm kitchen.

I roused myself from the comfort of Mrs Quigg's

My route was lower down the slopes of Temain Hill and further east than the present waymarked route, which keeps west when it leaves the forest and passes by the radio masts on the summit of Temain Hill.

The Legavannon Pot is a curious geological feature, a sudden chasm in the ground forming a deep gorge. There is a similar one, the Legananam Pot, about 2 miles to the south-west, also on the route of the Way.

turf fire and walked out again into the cold wind. A short way down the Dungiven road I turned off for the McCartney's farm, and I was soon comfortably installed by another warm fire in Mrs McCartney's sitting-room. In the past this had been a Guest Farm, but Mrs McCartney had discontinued taking guests. When I pleaded my necessity she had agreed to stretch a point and take me in, and I spent a very pleasant and comfortable night in her large hospitable farmhouse.

Day 3   Friday 30 March: to Moneyneaney

The Way is now routed through Dungiven, where accommodation is available, so it follows the road over the shoulder of Benbradagh (see map for Day 3).

The day began bright and dry, and at last the teasing wind had dropped. I took the road in good spirits, heading for the Legananam Pot. Passing this I turned right along the road made for the former U.S. Communications base on the eastern slopes of Benbradagh. After about a mile on this road I turned off into the bog, passing a small farm, where I took the opportunity to change my boots. I had two pairs of boots, a soft lightweight pair for hard surfaces, roads and forest tracks, and a heavier, stouter and more waterproof pair for bog and mountain. The lighter pair were more comfortable for my sore toe, so I wore them whenever I could. But now I was about to cross a long stretch of bog and mountain, so I decided to put on my heavier ones. It may seem unnecessary to call at a house to change one's boots. All I wanted, in fact, was a dry surface to sit on while I made the change, and I asked the farmer's wife if I might sit on her doorstep. She very obligingly brought me out a chair. I could easily enough have sat on the ground, but to avoid a wet bottom, this means unpacking and spreading out something waterproof.

Shod in my almost bogproof boots, and with the

27

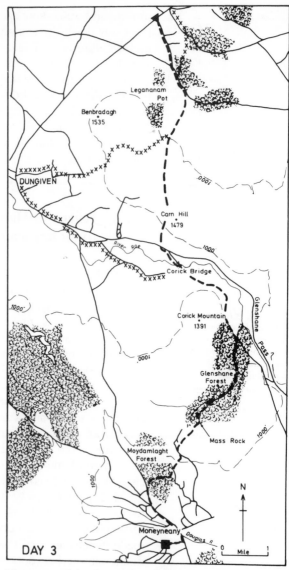

DAY 3

blessings of the farmer's wife, I strode off across the
bog in the direction of Carn Hill. The sun was shining
and the larks were singing; perhaps the spring was
coming at last.

At one point I passed what I thought was a dead

sheep. I paused and went to look at it. It was on its back, legs stuck stiffly in the air and its belly seemed swollen. Perhaps it had died in labour. As I went closer its head moved, and I saw that it was not dead but simply stuck on its back. It struggled to get up, but couldn't, so I approached it gingerly (I am not used to handling sheep), gave it a side-ways tug, and up it got and made off. My good turn for the day.

Hearing the larks singing in the clear air made me think of the Irish folk-tune, 'The Lark in the Clear Air'. I heard it played on a flute at the memorial service for Joey Glover which was held at the foot of Errigal mountain a few years ago. Joey, the founder–chairman of the North West Mountaineering Club, was shot by a gunman in Derry in November, 1976. He was not a political figure, and it is difficult to find any real motive for such a shooting, as in the case of other sad and meaningless acts of violence during the years of Ulster's troubles. Joey had a real passion for mountains. He had climbed Errigal nearly a hundred times, and there is now a plaque to his memory on a prominent rock on the way to the summit of that mountain. He would have been enthusiastic about the Ulster Way, and he would have walked it in considerably less time than I shall. I thought of him again when I reached the shoulder of Carn Hill and saw the Sperrins spread out before me, some of them still snow-capped. I could see the range of hills, including Sawel and Dart, that Joey christened 'The Sperrin Skyway'.

Details of the Sperrin Skyway may be found in *Irish Peaks,* ed. Joss Lynam (Constable, 1982) p. 222.

From Carn Hill I could hear the roar of lorries going up the Glenshane Pass. I descended towards the main road and just before reaching it I came across another sheep stuck on its back. This time I realised at once that it was not dead, and I was rather more adept about righting it. I crossed the main road and took a lane to Corrick bridge, and afterwards a muddy track running parallel to the Glenshane Pass on the south–east side of the River Roe, at this point only a mountain stream. The track led me eventually

On a later visit I saw the rock, a square block of stone clearly suitable to serve as an open air altar. One could easily imagine a congregation of faithful Roman Catholics in the Penal days of the early eighteenth century, gathered secretly in this remote and hidden glen, to receive the sacrament at the hands of an unregistered and forbidden priest, with a sentinel posted on the hillside above to keep watch for possible intruders. Alas, when I actually saw the altar it bore only an empty coca-cola bottle.

into Glenshane Forest. Here I had lunch—hot soup from my thermos flask, a piece of brown bread, an apple, a piece of cheese, and a few nuts and raisins—in a pleasant spot on the bank of the river. I was still wearing my heavy boots and my toe felt sore. I bathed my foot in the cold mountain stream—so cold it made my ankle ache—anointed it with Lanosil, and put on my lighter boots. The toe felt much better.

I went on up the forest track, following the stream, a pleasant winding route to the top of the Forest. On the stream I saw a heron, a dipper and a pair of mallard. I knew that there was a Mass Rock in this forest but I had no idea of its whereabouts, so I passed quite close to it without knowing. At night I learned from my host in Moneyneaney, who was a forester, that it was up at the top of the forest in a little glen below the fence, which I crossed on the way over the boggy mountainside to Moydamlaght Forest.

Descending the hillside towards the lower part of Moydamlaght Forest, I struck a fire-break which soon lead me to a broad, gravelled forest road. This took me to the 'Sruhanroe Walk', a most attractive winding path laid out by the Forestry Department as part of their amenities for visitors. The path, soft with fallen pine needles and very soothing to tired feet, led down the banks of a little stream to the picnic area at the entrance to the forest. From the entrance I took the road down to Moneyneaney, where I was able to buy two apples and some more cheese, provisions for my next two lunches.

I spent the night at a small guest-house, which I had seen listed in *All the Places to Stay in Northern Ireland*. My hostess, Mrs McKernan, worked during the day in nearby Draperstown, and her husband worked for the Forestry Department. She had prepared a casserole dish for me and was anxious that it might not be to my taste. She need not have worried. I am particulary fond of casserole dishes, and my appetite after a day in the keen March air was ready for most things. I was treated with genuine warmth and kindness, but the plan of the house was a little awkward for a guest. The bathroom was on the ground floor, off the kitchen. My bedroom was upstairs, and when I woke in the night and needed the bathroom, I had to find my way downstairs, through the sitting-room, dining-room and kitchen. I had no idea where the various light switches were, but fortunately I had placed my small torch close at hand, so I was able to find my way through the house without mishap.

Day 4   Saturday 31 March: to Cranagh

I am now well into the Sperrins and today I followed the route westward towards Gortin. I went up a winding track on to Crockmore. From the summit I had fine views all round me, to Lough Neagh and Slieve Gallion one way, to Benbradagh northwards, and westwards to Sawel and Dart. There were patches of snow at my feet, but the larks were singing again. For a time the hills were bathed in sunshine, though there were clouds in the west and on one of them I could see the brief gleam of a rainbow. I felt in buoyant spirits, and my sore toe was blessedly quiet. Then I thought of some of those who can no longer

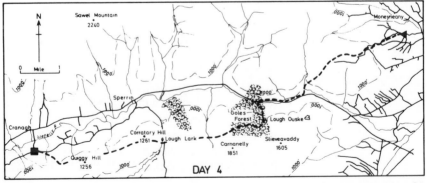

In the Sperrins, looking across the Glenelly River Valley to Sawel Mountain

share the keen joy of walking in the hills, and I held a brief half-hour of communion with dead friends. With Colin, my friend of college days, my walking companion in North Wales in the long-ago spring of 1936. We were both caught in a blizzard on Snowdon, an experience I have never forgotten. He was killed in the war a few years later.

I believe someone once described the Sperrins as 'turf floating on water'. I have certainly long thought of them as the 'sodden Sperrins', and for many years I rather avoided walking in them. But my prejudice against them, like most other prejudices, was based on one or two experiences only. Now that I know them better, I think that the Sperrin hills offer some delightful walking, and they enclose some of the most beautiful country in Ulster. But they are boggy and rough, and an attempt to take a beeline across the hills can be tedious. The 'official' Ulster Way seemed to follow the crests of the hills south of the Glenelly River—Slieveavaddy, Carnanelly, Mullaghbane, Corratary Hill and Quiggy Hill. I had already, on an exploring trip, gone past Lough Ouske up on to the slopes of Slieveavaddy, and found it very soggy going. So now, acting on the advice of Mr McKernan, my forester host, after descending to the road from Crockbank, I continued along it until I came to Goles Forest. I found a pleasant forest track here winding up beside a small stream and eventually I traversed the forest on to the side of Carnanelly. Crossing a saddle in the hills, heading west, I followed a stream down to Lough Lark. From here I climbed on to the flank of Corratarry Hill and pushed on towards Quiggy Hill. It was a tedious trudge over spongy ground, rough heather and tussocky grass. There were fine open views, but I was glad to get down at last to a tarred road, which I followed into Cranagh. Cranagh, down in the Glennelly River Valley, was off the main route, but the only way to find a lodging was to come down off the hills. Cranagh is only a small village, but it is on the scenic route from Drapers-town to Plumbridge, and it contains a modern and well-appointed Guest House, run by Mrs Conway. I was received with friendly warmth, given an excellent meal and I spent a comfortable night.

I am pleased to say that this route through Goles Forest has now been adopted by the Sports Council.

Day 5   Sunday 1 April:
to Lislap

It was raining in the morning when I started, and I set out in waterproof anorak and overtrousers. After a time the rain stopped, but soon it began to snow. I blenched at the thought of climbing up the spongy side of Clogherny Top to regain the crest of the hills and chose instead to follow the little by-road to Barnes Gap, there to regain the hills. The snow came on more heavily, and I found temporary shelter in

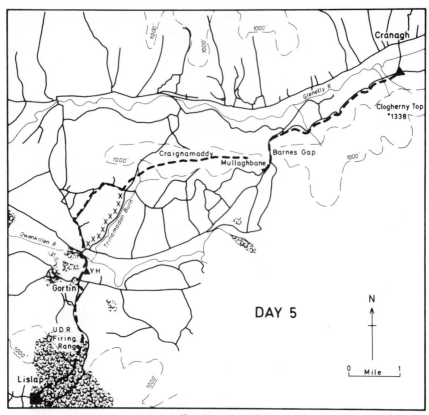

Barnes Gap offers a very convenient pass through the Sperrin hills and several minor roads converge there. It is not only convenient, it is also beautiful. The pass spills down with dramatic suddenness on the north side, and a stream cascades down with it. From the hills above the gap, on both sides, there are fine views over the surrounding countryside, especially to the north, where the highest range of the Sperrins extends along the Glennelly River.

the nulk of a ruined house. There was a small piece of ceiling still left, which gave me cover in one corner. I sat hunched up here on a truss of straw, like King Lear in his hovel on the heath, and drank a cup of soup from my flask by way of elevenses. I soon pushed on to Barnes Gap and climbed up the hillside to the west, heading for Gortin. The snow had ceased, but before long a fierce hail squall blew over the hills. I found at least partial shelter from its fury by pressing myself against the deep bank of a turf-cutting. Fortunately the worst of the squall was soon over and I went on over the boggy hillside. I stopped for lunch at a pile of polythene bags containing turf, where I found a convenient and not too sodden seat. Here I changed my soaked stockings for dry ones, and had just got them on when another squall blew up.

Now I had another problem. This section of the Ulster Way involves the corners of three O.S. maps. I had two of them, but I had forgotten that the route just crossed the corner of the third, the Tyrone section, and I had posted this one on ahead, together with a batch of others to be picked up at my stopping place near Derrygonnelly in West Fermanagh: I had to guess my way and somehow I got into the wrong by-road when I came off the hills, and made a wider circuit into Gortin than I need have done.

Although it was years since I had taken a photograph of any kind I decided to carry a camera with me on this walk, and the Sports Council encouraged me to take as many photos as I could. So I borrowed my wife's second-best camera (I thought the best was too heavy and too complicated), a Kodak *Instamatic*, and I did in fact take a lot of photos. I kept running out of film and had some trouble getting more, since I was not often passing a chemist's shop. There was one in Gortin, but it was Sunday. However, I had been given the names of a couple in Gortin who would help me, and I rang them the day before, asking them to buy some film for me. So I called now on Frank and Anne McGuigan in Main Street to collect the film. Anne brought me a welcome cup of coffee with a slice of apple tart, so I walked on fortified up the Burn Walk, a footpath made by the local council that follows the stream from the main street up to join the Gortin Gap road near the UDR firing range. As I went up the path I met a farmer who was looking out for his lambing ewes. He showed me a blood-stained patch on the grass where he said a lamb had been born less than an hour ago. The lamb, already on its feet, had moved on with its mother.

This friendly farmer also showed me how to get into the forest beside the firing range. Firing was

In Gortin village the old police barracks, just off the main street, has been converted into a Youth Hostel. This is open all the year round. Other accommodation may also be found in the village, which is a good centre for walking in the Sperrin country.

then in progress and I was a little alarmed at notices saying 'Do not pass this point when firing is in progress'. But the farmer gave me directions and told me that it was perfectly safe. The forest tracks were a little confusing. I took one wrong turn which led me up to a dead end in a turf bog, where I just had to turn round and re-trace my steps, but I finally came out on the side-road running towards Lislap, and I reached my night's lodging at Hillcrest Farm Guest House. Here I had a warm welcome from Mrs McFarland, and soon sat down to an excellent meal: soup, steak with whole potatoes, and lemon-meringue pie, followed by two cups of tea. This was a farm, with a farmyard and milking-parlour, and the dwelling house was warm and comfortable. There was an upstairs lounge with a fire, and my bedroom was just off this. I slept the just sleep of the tired walker who has battled through snow and hail and rain.

Day 6 Monday 2 April: to Letterbin

The Gortin Glen Forest Park was opened in 1967 and it contains over 1,000 acres of the much larger forest of Gortin Glen. It has a range of amenities for visitors, including a number of trails for walking, each marked with a colour code. There is also a wild-fowl sanctuary and an enclosure containing a small herd of Sika deer. The forest climbs the mountainside and at many points there are fine views over the Strule valley with the Donegal highlands beyond.

The day began dull, with mist on the hills and low cloud, but it gradually improved. A little snow had fallen in the night, making the pine trees in the forest look wintry. I took the road back to the Gortin Glen Forest Park and from the main entrance and parking area I followed the Ladies' View Trail (marked by brick-red arrows) up the Pollan Burn, an attractive, cascading, mountain stream, to My Ladies' View point, where there is a stone table with a distance chart. Then I took a green forest road for Glengawna, eventually passing the ruins of Glengawna Lodge, once no doubt a flourishing gentleman's residence. The forest walk was delightful and I felt again in buoyant spirits. I even began to sing, but soon a snow shower stopped my

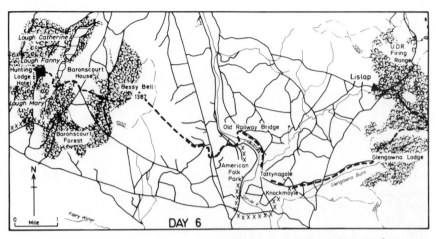

DAY 6

singing. As it came on I was passing a new house at Rossnamuck. I rang the bell and asked for shelter in the porch. Mrs McLaughlin invited me in and offered me a cup of tea. She turned out to be a keen walker and her husband was a keen bird watcher. They knew the local countryside well, so this chance visit was most fortunate for me, and I changed my route for the day in the light of their knowledge. I had previously reconnoitred a part of this area, trying to find a bridge over the river Strule that would take me towards Bessy Bell mountain on the way to Baronscourt. I had failed to find the bridge and so I was reconciled to going via the Stone Bridge, and thence by road to Baronscourt. But now I was told exactly where to find the old railway bridge, and I could see the beckoning summit of Bessy Bell in the distance. So I changed course, turned right at Knockmoyle, and took a little bog road to Tattynagole. Passing a steep bank at one point, I found a young lamb which had fallen through the mesh wire fence at the top into the road. Its mother was plaintively bleating above, and I was able to restore the lost lamb to her care.

My route followed the road running north alongside the Strule River. In one of the fields by the river I saw a flock of wild geese. The weather was still

The S.C. route goes via the Stone Bridge in order to include the Ulster-American Folk Park at Camphill. This park, which has an information centre and a café, commemorates the historical links between Ulster and America. It contains the Mellon Homestead, the restored cottage where Thomas Mellon was born in 1813, together with a schoolhouse, a barn, a forge and other buildings, both Irish and American. Admission is 50p for adults, and the park is open in summer (May-August) from 11.00 until 6.30, in winter September-April) from 10.30 to 4.30. But from November to February it is closed on Saturdays, Sundays and public holidays.

37

My Lady's Viewpoint in Gortin Glen Forest Park

showery, so I found shelter in a small copse to eat my lunch. Not long afterwards I came upon the bridge, an old railway bridge that had holes in some places but was still negotiable on foot. On the other side, near what seemed to be an old railway cottage, I found a sign reading: 'Trespassers will be prosecuted. E. M. Dunlop.'

I was really delighted that I was now heading for Bessy Bell. Not only was this a mountain that I had never climbed before, but I was charmed by its name. Most mountains have masculine-sounding names: Everest, Snowdon, Ben Nevis, Errigal; Bessy Bell, and her sister hill, Mary Gray, were apparently named by the Stewarts, Dukes of Abercorn, after the heroines of a Scottish ballad. They are only modest hills—Bessy Bell, the higher, is only 1387 ft.—but their names are memorable.

I crossed the main Omagh Road and made for Gortinagin. Here I found a track leading upwards, but it soon petered out and then it was a heavy, slushy slog over soft turf, rushes, heather and bog, up to the last rise of Bessy Bell. But when I reached the top the view was beautiful. The weather had cleared and I looked out over immense open stretches of cloud-dappled hill and plain. I could see Omagh clearly, and the Sperrins wreathed in soft cloud, and I looked north–west into Donegal. Errigal was in shadow, but I could see snow gleaming on Slieve Snaght. To the south–west lay Lough Erne. Bessy Bell may be only a humble hill, but because of its position it commands a superb view of Ulster countryside.

Baronscourt Forest runs down the west side of Bessy Bell and much of it is leased to the Department of Agriculture, but Baronscourt House, a large Georgian mansion, is still the private home of the Duke of Abercorn. There are terraced Italian gardens, some fine trees and three lakes.

Now to my delight, since the route was entirely new to me, I discovered a good firm track right beside the summit, leading down through the forest to Baronscourt. To complete my day a deer leapt out on to the road about five yards in front of me. At first I thought it was a big dog. There is a large herd of deer in the Baronscourt estate, and I learnt later that the herd had recently been culled. Four hundred of them had been shot and put in freezers, later to be sent to London.

When I emerged from the forest I enquired my way at one of the houses on the estate and was told I might go through to Letterbin past Lough Fanny and Lough Mary. I was to spend the night at Letterbin, where what had once been a National School, and then a Nature Reserve Centre, was now being turned into the Hunters' Lodge Hotel. The new hotel was not yet open, but the proprietor, to whom I had previously written, had kindly agreed to take me in, and he gave me a bed in his own private flat.

Day 7 Tuesday 3 April: to Menacloy

There was quite a sharp frost last night, and the morning was bright, clear and windless, ideal for

39

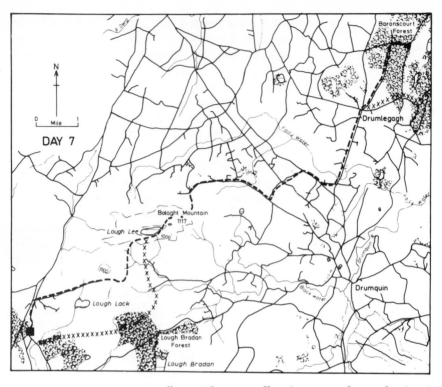

walking. When I proffered payment for my food and lodging Mr McSorley would take nothing. I set out for Drumleggagh, following a minor road, straight but pleasant, with birch trees growing each side. The melting rime on the branches sparkled in the sun. I could see Bessy Bell to my left and Bolaght Mountain in front. In the post office at Drumleggagh, which was also a shop, my eye was attracted by a ripe red tomato. I bought it to eat for lunch and put it in the breast pocket of my anorak for safety. The power of the sun was increasing. I sat in a sunny corner on some steps to shed a jersey and re-pack my rucksack. With my usual absent-mindedness I put the anorak under me to sit on and promptly squashed the ripe tomato. It took me about twenty minutes to clear up the resulting mess in my anorak pocket. Then I went on down another straight road to cross a river called Fairy Water. Fairy Water did not quite live up to the charm of its name. It had recently been cleaned and dredged at the point where I crossed it, and there were piles of mud on the banks, so it was not exactly fairy-like. But in a field near the river I saw four swans, and the name began to echo in my mind. I started a snatch of verse:

> I saw four swans in a field
> By Fairy Water . . .

but I got no further than these two lines. Yet the place names of my journey continued to haunt me, and I began to compose what eventually became 'A Song of the Ulster Way'. Today I got as far as the first two verses.

> I took a walk in Ulster
> The Way is long to tell
> I went by Fairy Water
> And over Bessy Bell.

> Lough Fanny and Lough Mary
> Hid many a quiet fin
> As I passed by their waters
> To sleep at Letterbin.

The warmth of the sun was increasing and I felt a sense of spring at last. I actually saw a primrose, though it was a rather scruffy one, and then a few celandines. I was still following roads, but I had them almost to myself. Only a very occasional car passed me. Now I went up past Kilmore Lodge towards the flank of Bolaght mountain, still on a minor road. It was unfenced and offered splendid views away to the Donegal Highlands. I could see Castlederg in the plain below, and the Sperrins away to the north-east. I had brown mountainy bog on my left hand and wide sweeping views on the right.

At lunch time I had reached the end of the road, near a small farm. A hailstorm was threatening now, so I asked the farmer, who was working in a field nearby if I might take shelter in his turf shed. He told me I was welcome to do so and I sat on some old turf bags and lunched under cover. Afterwards I walked up into the bog on Bolaght Mountain, following the convenient red posts set up to guide fishermen to Lough Lee. After walking eight or nine miles on hard roads, I was beginning to feel the pressure on my sore toe, so that I was very glad to get on to soft boggy ground again. It was easy to find Lough Lee, but after this I was heading for Lough Lack, which was not yet visible. I took a compass bearing to make sure that I was heading in the right direction. Then I caught sight of a forest track in a newly planted part of Lough Bradan Forest. I headed for this and got on to a newly laid soft black gravel track. But I was uncertain which way to turn. Should I go left or right? I went right, and a few minutes later a car appeared with two men in it. What extraordinary good luck. I stopped the car and asked my way. I was told to turn round and go in the opposite direction, which I promptly did, and finally Lough Lack came into view. At last I could see the ground ahead of me and I decided to keep above Lough Lack, and take the green road to Scaghey. This was a pleasant track with open views all round. I could see Lough Erne, and away in the distance, the outline of Ben Bulben. The map marks a Chamber Grave on this track, but I missed it, and finally hit the road from Castlederg to Kesh. I walked along the road for a short distance until I came to Mrs Gormley's farm house at Menacloy. This was simply a farm-house, not a guest house, but Mrs Gormley had kindly agreed to take me in, and she treated me like an honoured guest.

Day 8 Wednesday 4 April: to Magho

I woke up at 6.30 after a comfortable night in an elegant bedroom. I remembered my boots that I had left drying by the fire. I was a little anxious about them, in case they had dried too quickly. A walker must look after his boots as a cowboy looks after his horse. So I went down to the sitting-room to fetch them. There I found my hostess sleeping on the divan. Clearly she had given me her own bed, though she tried to tell me that she often slept in the sitting-room. Her mother, Mrs Gordon, who lived with her on the farm, was equally obliging. When I said that I seemed to have left my shaving brush behind, she promptly produced one and made me a present of it.

I had twenty miles to do to-day, mainly on minor roads, through Pettigoe to Rosscor Bridge near Belleek. Here Mr Neal, my host for the night, had kindly agreed to pick me up and take me on to the Guest House run by his wife. I had stayed with the Neals before, on one of my exploratory trips, and had come to know them. The guest house was on the Enniskillen–Belleek Road, a very comfortable modern bungalow called Shangra-La.

I passed near Drumskinney Stone Circle, so I went to take a look at it. It was a small but very neat

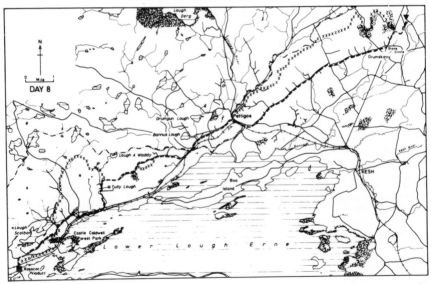

and well-kept circle of ancient stones. The notice board dated it between 1,600 and 1,200 BC. The notice also said that further information would be supplied by the caretaker. Out of curiosity I called on him at a farmhouse nearby, but I very soon discovered that he knew less about the stone circle than I did myself, so I went on my way.

I was walking on a minor road through Corlave to Pettigoe. There was hardly any traffic, so it was quite pleasant walking, and I had glimpses of Lough Erne. At Corlave I noticed a call-box and remembered that I was due to phone Walter Love and report my progress. I found I had no change for the call-box, but I saw what appeared to be a travelling shop not far off. I got change there, and met the only stranger I had so far come across who knew something about the Ulster Way. After a brief chat with Walter Love I pushed on towards Pettigoe. A passing car stopped and offered me a lift. I had to decline, of course, though I was grateful for the offer, but at the last minute it occurred to me that I might let the driver take my rucksack, without breaking my walk. So I asked him to leave it at the Custom Post in Pettigoe, where I picked it up later. Pettigoe is a small town right astride the border, and the Ulster Way runs for a mile or two in Co. Donegal before crossing the Waterfoot river back into Co. Fermanagh. The bridge over this river had been blown up some years back, but I knew it was possible to cross over the old railway bridge. Near the bridge I passed an Irish Army patrol, but they showed no curiosity in my movements, and nobody asked me where I was going. After crossing the border I took a by-road and then a forest track to Tullychurry. The walking was pleasant and the roads empty of traffic, and the roadsides tree-lined. The forest was mostly pine, but the country was hilly and undulating, and I had some good open views over Lough Erne.

I had to come down to the main road at Leggs Post Office, but I soon turned off it again to pass

This section of the way has now been re-routed to avoid the long stretch of road, and waymarked by the Fermanagh District Council. The new route is shown on the map for Day 8.

Pettigoe is the starting point for a planned extension of the Ulster Way round the county of Donegal. The trail runs north to Lough Derg, which contains the island of St Patrick's Purgatory, a famous place of pilgrimage. Passing Lough Derg the trail moves north–west into the Blue Stack mountains. Some of it is already waymarked.

Lough Scolban, only just glimpsed on my right, and Castle Caldwell church. I came down once more to the main Belleek road, but turned off it for Rosscor Bridge, where Mr Neal met me in his car. After twenty miles, nearly all on roads, I was very pleased to see him and ready for the pleasures of the journey's end. First the great relief of lifting the rucksack off my back and dumping it in the car. Then at Shangra-La I was able to shed my boots and step into a hot bath. After that I sat down to a delicious meal of steak and onions. Only one thing marred the pleasures of rest and food and warmth. I had expected to find a parcel awaiting me, the parcel I had posted to myself from Coleraine nine days before, containing clean shirts and socks, but even more important, the vital maps that I needed for the next stages of the Way. I went to bed that night feeling a little dispirited and worried. How could I go on without those maps? But in the night I began to think of ways round my difficulty, and in the morning I had partly recovered my spirits.

This section of the Way has been re-routed and now includes a part of Castle Caldwell Forest Park, which consists of two long peninsulas stretching out into Lough Erne. The park is a wild-fowl reserve, where many species of duck and geese may be seen. At the entrance gate stands the 'fiddler's stone', set up in 1770 to the memory of a fiddler who fell out of a barge when drunk and was drowned.

Day 9   Thursday 5 April: to Doagh

I spent a good part of the morning telephoning. First I tried to trace the parcel. I phoned the Post Office in Coleraine. They tried to help and did what they could by phoning Belfast and Enniskillen, but there was no real result of their enquiries. I then rang Nigel Jess of the Northern Ireland Tourist Board to see if he could suggest someone in Enniskillen who might help me. He suggested John Crighton of the Fermanagh District Council. I rang him and he put me in touch with Mrs Ruth Blair, who kindly agreed to get me new maps and bring them out to Shangra-La.

I had decided that I would skip the stretch of

The Lakeland Way is the name given to the stretch of the Ulster Way that runs from Magho to Belcoo, passing through Fermanagh lakeland scenery. The country is hilly and wooded, with many little mountain tarns, and there is a rich variety of wild flowers.

45

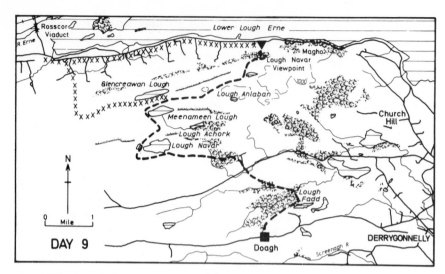

At Magho car park there is a walking man sign indicating the Ulster Way. The path climbs up from the main road (the A46 from Beleek to Enniskillen) and the car park is about 7 miles from Beleek, about 13 from Enniskillen.

There is a long stretch of main road to be walked from Rosscor Viaduct to Magho car park. To avoid this an alternative route has been devised, branching off from the road about 2 miles from the viaduct. (See map for Day 9).

main road from Rosscor Bridge to Magho car park (I should have gone back to the point where I was picked up last night) and start late on the Lakeland Way, a stretch of the Ulster Way that begins at Magho. Then at 11.15, the postman arrived at the house with my missing parcel. I phoned Ruth Blair at once and was able to stop her coming out. So I had lost most of the morning and a small piece of the Ulster Way. This latter did not trouble my conscience much, because it was only a stretch of main road.

I left Magho Car Park soon after noon and went gently up the steep slope. There are many stone steps, mossy and green. Seats are provided all the way up and there are fine views out over Lough Erne. The path winds through mixed woodland—hazel, birch, holly and other trees—though ash predominates on the limestone soil. It is a steep and narrow path, but there were primroses growing plentifully on the mossy banks at the sides. Why is the primrose associated with the downward slope to damnation? Shakespeare makes Polonius speak of 'the primrose way to the everlasting bonfire', and Laertes contrasts 'the primrose path of dalliance'

46

with 'the steep and thorny way to heaven'. Why should the devil have all the primroses as well as all the best tunes? Here was a primrose path leading upwards to heaven. It was narrow and steep, demanding energy to climb, just like the traditional conception of the path of righteousness, and yet it was sprinkled bountifully with primroses.

I was in a state of mild euphoria after my parcel had arrived. Before that it seemed as if all my carefully laid plans were being wrecked. Now I was back on an even keel. The enforced rest in the comfort of Shangra-La, instead of striding out on the road at 9.00 am, had been good for my sore toe. So I was in excellent spirits as I climbed up my primrose path. My thoughts flowed freely and I talked to myself.

I felt again the warmth of Ulster hospitality. I thought of Mrs Gormley sleeping on the settee in her living room, so that I could have her bed, and of the general decency and friendliness of Ulster people. Of all the isolated call-boxes I have passed so far on this journey, not one has been vandalized. Once in Willesden, London, I was trying to make an urgent call, and out of six boxes near to me, not one was fit to be used. And yet the world thinks of Ulster as a savage and violent place. The violence and savagery are there too, of course. When I was on top of Bessy Bell, that lovely mountain, looking down on distant Omagh, tranquil in the evening sunshine, I remembered that a 300 lb bomb had exploded there the day before. There is violence and savagery; but there is also peace and friendliness in Ulster, and such tranquil beauty in the landscape.

At the top of my climb, at the Lough Navar viewpoint, the Lakeland Way turns west and before long joins up with a forest road. It was a luxury to be on a waymarked route. The markers were stout posts with orange arrows on them, and I found it necessary to look carefully at the direction of the arrows. In the softer boggy patches the marks of

The Lough Navar viewpoint has a car park and cars may reach it from the south through Church Hill or Derrygonnelly. There is a useful map-table in the car park indicating the direction of the views. This is certainly a fine viewpoint, commanding a wide expanse of Lough Erne, a part of the Donegal coast, and many mountains.

On the Lakeland Way—the view over Lower Lough Erne from Navar Forest, above Magho

boots showed that the path is being quite well used, and so far it is pleasingly free of litter. But today I had the whole Way entirely to myself. The beautiful little loughs seemed lonely and serene: even the birds seemed scarce. I saw only one mallard and a pair of smaller ducks.

At Melly's Rock I visited the Sweat House. A help-ful notice has been erected here, explaining its purpose. It was a kind of primitive Sauna. A large turf fire was lit in the little stone house and then rushes were laid over the floor, and thus a sweating heat was provided for the patient. It was used to treat rheumatism, arthritis and similar troubles.

I reached Doagh car park soon after six, and here I had to turn off the Way to get to my lodging for the night. I was staying at an unlisted guest house in Derrygonnelly village, 3¼ miles away down the county road. I was quite ready to beg a lift, since this was not part of my route, but although two cars and two vans passed me going the other way, not one vehicle of any kind came past in my direction. I made the best speed I could, knowing that I was late, and thinking that my evening meal might be shrivelling in the oven. But my hostess had prepared a cold meal for me so no harm was done. I had chicken and ham, cold mashed potato and a tomato, followed by bread and butter and straw-berry jam, and a few cakes. I ate in the kitchen where there was a full tea-pot on the oil-burning stove. When I retired for the night I found two hot-water bottles in my bed. One of them was a stone jar, such as I have not encountered since my childhood.

Day 10 Friday 6 April:
to Belcoo

I was anxious to avoid the additional mileage back up the road to the Lakeland Way this morning, since I knew I would have to go off the route again at the other end, so last night I arranged for a local publican, who also acted as a taxi-driver, to drive me up this morning to the Doagh car park. He said the charge would be £1. So, after an early breakfast, I was driven up through a thick mist to find the sun beginning to break through on the hills. When Patrick McGovern, my driver (farmer, publican and man of many skills) dropped me on the road, he at first declined to accept any payment but, since we had already agreed on a fee, I insisted that he should take it.

I began to walk and realised at once that I had left my walking stick behind in Derrygonnelly. I had failed to check off the items on my check-card this morning. I spent some time wondering how I might

recover the stick. Could I phone the local Post
Office, since the house where I had stayed had no
phone? But it was very unlikely that I would strike a
call-box anywhere. I thought of stopping a car, but
no cars came by, so I decided to go ahead and try
my luck at the end of the day in Belcoo.

To many walkers a stick is an unnecessary en-
cumbrance, but I have grown used to carrying a
stick, which I find useful in many ways. The one I
had left behind had been my companion for some
thirty years. It was an African hardwood, light but
strong, which I originally acquired in Kampala.

The mist dispersed, the sun came through, and
there was a fresh early morning feel about the Lakeland Way that made walking delightful. I soon

forgot about the loss of my stick and began to sing and whistle, and recite aloud snatches of poetry. I passed the Big Dog and Little Dog section of the Way, one of the most beautiful. The Dogs are hills, and beneath them lie the lovely loughs, Lough Formal and Lough Doo. I took several photos.

After passing through Ballintempo Forest I reached the county road near Holywell before 4.00 pm. I pushed straight on down the road to Belcoo, though my night's lodging was to be at Corralea, where a new Guest House was soon to open on the shore of Lough MacNean Upper. Peter Catterall, the proprietor, had kindly agreed to take me in, though he was not yet really ready for guests. I made enquiries in the Belcoo Post Office whether any vans would be coming from Derrygonnelly, or whether there were any cars for hire in Belcoo, but there was nothing doing. I was told to try Blacklion across the border in Co. Cavan. I walked on into Blacklion, and there I learnt that there was a car for hire, but it had gone to Sligo. I consoled myself with a bottle of Guinness and walked back to Belcoo, thinking I would try the Blacklion car again in the morning, and kill two birds with one stone by getting the driver to rescue my stick and also take some of the contents of my rucksack on to my next destination at Swanlinbar, so that I would have a lighter load on the Cuilcagh mountains.

From Belcoo I had to return up the Garrison Road to Corralea. Since I was going back on my tracks, I decided to hitch a lift. Fortunately there were some cars going my way. The first two ignored my lifted thumb, but the third one stopped. It was, in fact, Peter Catterall, my host, but he didn't reveal this until we reached his house. When I asked him if he knew Peter Catterall, all he replied was, 'Yes'. Was this Lancashire humour? I learnt later that he had been born and brought up in Blackburn, and he still retained his Lancashire accent, though he had been working as a vet in Ulster since 1960.

His new house was lovely and very luxurious. I am writing now in a large lounge with central heating and a log fire in the grate. There are fine views over Lough MacClean. There are several bedrooms downstairs, and a long patio above. My bedroom includes a private lavatory and washbasin, and a separate shower with a tiled floor, where the light is combined with an extractor fan. I dined with the family and was treated with the warmest friendliness and hospitality.

Day 11 Saturday 7 April: to Swanlinbar

Since I had already walked to Blacklion, I had no hesitation in accepting a lift from Peter Catteral in the morning. He dropped me there about nine and I made further efforts to contact the local 'taxi' driver. I am a natural early riser, and even after living in Ireland for twenty years I have to remind myself that life does not begin in many small Irish towns and villages until after ten in the morning. There was certainly little sign of life in Blacklion at nine. I knew that the taxi was to be found at the Bush Bar, and there were, in fact, two cars standing outside the door. I knocked at the door, and waited. Dead silence. I knocked again and listened. Silence once again. I hammered on the door, and three houses up the road a man in pyjamas opened the window and stuck his head out. I approached him and explained what I was looking for. He told me that the best way to rouse the people in the Bush Bar would be to telephone them, and he suggested that I should go up to the Gardai station and ask them to telephone. I did so—it was close by—and rang the bell at the door, once, twice, three times. Dead silence again in Blacklion. Near the Gardai station there was an Irish Army patrol, manning a check-

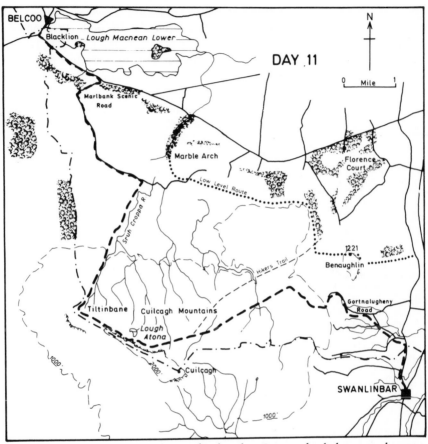

point at the border. I consulted them on how to rouse the Gardai, but they advised me to try the Post Office, which was now open across the road. I went across and an obliging girl tried to phone the Bush Bar for me, but she got no answer.

The next section of the Way was one that I knew almost nothing about. I had seen the Cuilcagh range from a distance but that was all, so I was anxious to get some local advice about the best way to go. Before knocking at the Bush Bar I had found a shop open and enquired there if there was someone who knew the local countryside and could advise me on the approach to the Cuilcaghs. They told me that

53

An alternative route, avoiding Belcoo and passing along the shore of Lough MacNean Lower and up the Cladagh River to Marble Arch, has now been way-marked by the Fermanagh D.C. From Marble Arch this route will go south to the Cat's Hole and then east towards the south end of Florencecourt Forest Park and over Benaughlin (see map for Day 11). This route will avoid the Cuilcagh ridge which can be difficult in bad weather.

There is now a 'hikers' trail' from the edge of Florencecourt Forest Park to the foot of Cuilcagh, way-marked with yellow painted posts. This could be a useful escape route for anyone overtaken by mist or storm. The northern approach to the Cuilcagh ridge is over a wide, featureless upland bog, a true wilderness, and no one should venture on it without a compass.

Harry Smith was my man, and somebody obligingly went to fetch him. While the girl in the Post Office was still getting no reply from the Bush Bar, Harry Smith arrived. He was very friendly and ready to help, but he told me that the man who really knew the country I was going through was Basil Ellot, the farmer at Border Farm. So I decided to forget about the Bush Bar and push on for Border Farm. Here I received a most friendly welcome, and Basil Ellot was my good Samaritan today. He not only gave me advice on the route, but he helped me with my other problems. I used his telephone to ring Patrick McGovern, my taxi-driver in Derrygonnelly. He was out, but I left a message with a woman's voice at the other end of the phone to ask him to bring on my stick and a parcel from Border Farm to Swanlinbar. I left a parcel at the farm to lighten my load for the Cuilcagh climb. I was a little apprehensive about the route ahead of me because it was quite unknown, but I realised there would be a good stretch of bog.

So I set off along the road to Florencecourt with a lightened load and in good spirits. Basil Ellot had advised me to take the Marlbank Loop road rather than trying to cut across country, so I followed this road as far as the little ruined and abandoned Marble Arches Primary School. On the road I noticed some ash saplings in the hedge, and I wondered about cutting one to replace my missing stick. Then I thought it would be wasting time to cut a stick for just one day. Finally I saw such a good one that I did stop and cut it. It turned out to be in-valuable later in the day.

About mid-morning I passed such a snug-looking hay-barn near a small farm, that I couldn't resist knocking at the door and asking if I might drink my coffee there. It was not raining, but there was a sharp cold wind. A woman came to the door when I knocked. She looked a little surprised at my request, but readily agreed, so I drank my coffee in comfort, well sheltered from the wind with my back against a warm bank of hay.

Although Florencecourt is somewhat off the route of the Way it is well worth a visit. The large Georgian mansion, once he home of the Cole family of Enniskillen, is now held by the National Trust and is open from April to September, from 2.00–6.00 pm. The Forest Park is open every day of the year from 10.00 am to half an hour before sunset.

At the abandoned school, I cut off into the fields and headed up the Sruh Croppa river valley. It was fairly easy going over small fields and small ditches, but later I came to heathery hills and bog. I lunched on a hillside, finding what shelter I could from the wind. Below me in the valley was a sheep lying very still. A grey crow cawed and flew close over the sheep, but it made no move. A little later two men and a dog, presumably looking for lambing sheep, came up to it. The sheep then got up and revealed a new-born lamb, still wobbly on its legs.

As I went on, the Cuilcagh ridge came into sight, dramatically covered in snow. The clouds were increasing behind me, and they looked ominously dark, but I thought that I could surely have no trouble following the ridge, once I had climbed on to it. My plan was to ascend the western end and walk along to Cuilcagh Mountain (2,188 ft) at the eastern end, then to descend and walk across the bog to pick up the Gortnalughany road. I reached the top of Tiltinbane (1,881 ft) soon after 3.00 and began to walk along the ridge. Almost at once it started to snow, but I decided to push on, thinking that I could follow the ridge even in poor visibility. Soon I was floundering in deep snow up to my knees, with drifts here and there much deeper. Now I thanked God I had a stick. I was able to probe the drifts ahead of me before I plunged into them. Sometimes I failed to touch bottom with the stick, and worked round another way. The snow ceased for a short time, then started again and turned into a blizzard. The cold increased and the visibility was reduced to a few yards. My gloves were wet, my hands numb, and I became quite uncertain of my direction. There seemed to be deep, rocky crevasses all around me. I managed to get out my compass and I found that I was going more west than east. For a time I was worried, even a little frightened. I realised that I must abandon my plan of following the ridge, and get off the mountain in the direction of the road. But there was nothing except the compass to give me any indication of direction, and all around me were forbidding clefts, cliffs and crevasses. I couldn't seem to find a promising slope to work my way down. Finally I got on to one and had a glimpse of snowy ground beneath me. I was unsure how steep a drop there might be below, but I worked my way cautiously down, feeling great relief at getting off the ridge. The snow ceased again, but visibility remained very poor. Finally I got a dim impression of Benaughlin in the distance, and I made a beeline for it, as far as I could across heavy bog. The going was very wet in places. There were some deep gulleys with swollen streams rushing down. I was in a fairly sodden state, but still relieved at being safely off the mountain. I never even saw the peak of Cuilcagh, which I was originally aiming for. After nearly two hours of bog-trotting I became aware of turf stacks in front of me—a welcome sign of civilisation. Soon I found a green turf-track and this led me to the tarred road. Walkers usually try to escape from tarred roads, but I was heartily relieved to see this one. Now I knew where I was, and could find my way to Swanlinbar. I celebrated by emptying the water out of my boots and putting on a pair of dry socks. Then I marched on down the road. I was now making a detour from the line of the Ulster Way to reach Swanlinbar, so when I heard an unexpected car behind me, after I had walked a mile or two, I hitched a lift to my lodging in the town.

The S.C. route has now been changed to take in Swanlinbar because it is possible to find accommodation here.

The parcel of clothing I had left at the Border Farm had not yet arrived, so I could not change, but I had a wash and drank some welcome cups of tea. Before long there was a ring at the door and Basil Ellot was there, bringing me everything, including my missing stick. Patrick McGovern had brought it as far as the Border Farm and then Basil brought it all on. Neither would accept any payment for petrol.

There was a great contrast between my

accommodation tonight and the luxury of Corralea. This was an old dilapidated house, with large rooms, difficult to heat. There was no carpet on the bare boards of the stairs. There was a fire in my bedroom, but the bed was not made up until later. In the bathroom there was a large gap at the window, letting in cold air. I had my meal at a table in the corner of the kitchen, where there was a solid fuel stove, but it barely heated the large lofty room. I enjoyed my supper, nonetheless—soup, steak with potatoes and carrots, followed by plain custard and tea.

Day 12   Sunday 8 April:
to Keady Orlit

As I left the house this morning it began to rain. I spent ten minutes in the shelter of a shop doorway unpacking my rucksack and getting my overtrousers and yellow anorak on. I bought an apple and an orange for lunch. It rained for about two hours, but I was quite happy in my oilskins. After yesterday today was an easy day on by-roads. I crossed the border by a lane running towards Drumbrughas, where there was a footbridge over the Blackwater. At Springtown crossroads, I found a convenient hay-barn to sit in while I drank my morning coffee. Then I followed the Doon Scenic Route over the shoulder of Molly

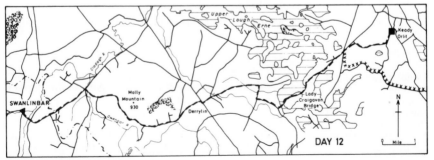

Mountain (another feminine mountain) to Derrylin. Here it would normally be well worth turning aside for the Doon Scenic View Point, which is signposted. This commands a fine view over Upper Lough Erne and its many islands, but today low cloud hid the view, so I went straight on. I was facing into a raw easterly wind all day, and I began to wonder if the spring would ever come. I started composing a complaint in verse.

> O late, late is the season
> Hungry the cows and sheep.
> April, you thieving borrower
> How many more bleak days
> Will you borrow from snow-cold March?

> The fields are brown and lifeless,
> The buds are closed on the trees,
> Will we ever hear the cuckoo?
> Will the swallows ever come?

This was not very inspired poetry, and I never completed the poem, but it reflects my mood at the time.

I reached Derrylin at lunchtime, so I walked into the bar at the Mount View Hotel, which seemed to be open, although it was Sunday. When I asked for a bottle of Guinness in my unmistakeably English voice, I thought I noticed a sudden rather ominous silence in the room where there had been a buzz of conversation. Was this perhaps a Republican venue, and did they think I might be an SAS man? The proprietor asked me if I was on holiday, and I told him briefly what I was doing. I mentioned that my walk was being sponsored, and he asked to see my sponsorship card. I didn't have one, so I showed him instead my Senior Citizen's travel concession card, which seemed to be the only proof of identity that I had in my wallet. He seemed satisfied with this, and gradually conversation resumed again in the bar as I sat eating my lunch. No one else asked me any questions.

After leaving Derrylin I crossed Upper Lough Erne by the Lady Craigavon Bridge. From Drumgruff Cross

I went to Keady Orlit because I had found hospitality there. I was somewhat off the line of the S.C. route which goes further south (see map for Day 12).

58

I cut across fields to a small bog road that finally brought me out to Keady Orlit. Here I received a very warm welcome from Mrs McAdam, warm in spirit and also physically warm. Her small pre-fabricated Council house was one of the snuggest I stayed in.

Day 13   Monday 9 April:
to Eshywulligan

This was not one of my better days. Soon after I set out it began to pour with rain. I asked permission to

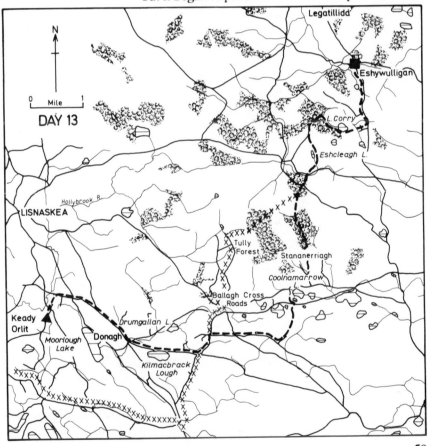

shelter and get my oilskins on in the porch of a
house I was passing. There I was watched by a
fascinated small boy. I walked through the heavy
rain to Donagh, where I sheltered briefly in a shop
and bought some food for lunch. Then I set off
again and took the wrong road, as a result of some
careless map-reading. I soon realised I was wrong
and tried to work back on to the right route. I should
have reached Ballagh Cross, but instead I found
myself at Knockawaddy, on a very minor road. I
knocked at the door of a small farmhouse, where I
was given a most friendly welcome by an elderly
couple. The farmer directed me across the fields to
the Rosslea road near Lough Drumaa, and from here
I was able to work back on to the right route and to
enter Strannaneriagh Forest near Mount Darby. But I
made a clumsy entrance to the forest, missing the
footpath and having to fight my way through the
trees to the forest track which I knew was there.
After this things went better, though I was on unfamiliar ground. I found my way by winding forest
tracks past Lough Escleagh and Lough Corry to the
crossroads at Eshywulligan. I found this a fascinating
name and worked it into my 'Song of the Ulster Way'.
From here I had to go off the Way again for a couple
of miles to Legatillida—another fascinating name. As
I trudged off, a little reluctantly, feeling the weight
of my rucksack, I heard the unexpected sound of a
car behind me. I raised my thumb and the driver of
a small van stopped and gave me a lift. A stroke of
luck to end a rather dismal day, though the rain had
ceased in the afternoon.

Day 14   Tuesday 10 April:
to Lough na Blaney Bane

I was less lucky this morning and had to walk back
to Eshywulligan crossroads. One car did in fact pass

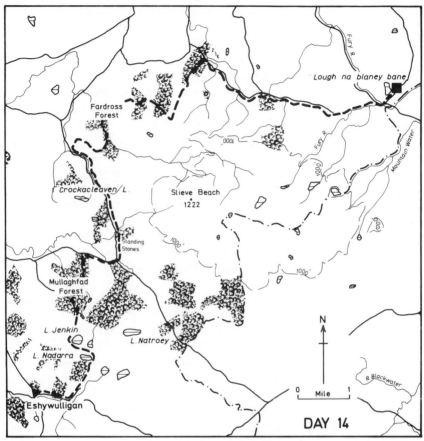

Fardross
Forest

Lough na blaney bane

Fury R.

Fury R.

Mountain Water

1000'

1000'

1000'

1000'

Crockacleaven L.

Slieve Beach
1222

Standing
Stones

1000'

1000'

Mullaghfad
Forest

L. Jenkin

L. Natroey

L. Nadarra

R. Blackwater

N

0   Mile   1

Eshywulligan

DAY 14

me, but I reacted too slowly and didn't manage to
stop it. After a short stretch of road, I took a forest
track leading up through boggy moorland towards
Mullaghfad Forest. It was a grey misty damp
morning, but not actually raining. There was still no
growth of spring grass, and I watched a group of
melancholy black cows eating the hay that a farmer
had just brought to them. But later I heard a single
cheerful lark.

My forest road had a pleasant sanded surface, soft
and smooth under the feet, much to be preferred to
the large and lumpy gravel that is found on some
forest roads. I find myself judging all roads by their

texture as felt underfoot. My favourite is the 'green' road. I passed Lough Jenkin and the observation tower (for forest fire watching) on Jenkin Hill. This tower made a useful landmark for me, and when I reached it I climbed up to the observation platform to get a better view of the route ahead. I managed to take the right tracks through Mullaghfad Forest, which I had not been in before and which pleased me considerably. I had a stretch of minor road and then I entered Fardross Forest. I was slowly working north-east, close to the Fermanagh-Cavan border, in the general direction of Clogher. At the entrance to Fardross Forest I had my lunch in some deserted farm buildings, and then went on following a pleasant green track beside a stream, with birch trees at one side and conifers on the other. At one point a red squirrel crossed the road, a creature I have not seen for many years. I emerged from Fardross Forest to follow minor roads eastwards towards Lough na Blaney Bane. I had arranged to stay the night at Kilrudden Guest Farm. This is three miles off the Way, but Mrs McKenna, my hostess, had very kindly agreed to pick me up in her car at the Lough. This was a lonely and remote section with no signposts on the minor roads. At one point I met three children coming home from school. I asked them how far it was to Lough na Blaney Bane. 'Haven't a clue,' the eldest replied. I thought they must be an ignorant lot of omadhauns not to know their own countryside, but I discovered later that this Lough is not known locally by this name, which I got from my map. It is simply called Lough Cavan. A pity, because Lough na Blaney Bane is a much more musical name. I retained it for my 'Song'.

At one point on my lonely, deserted road, I passed what had once been a small National School. I saw the date, 1859, over the door. It was now clearly a private house and I knocked on the door to check on my route. A small boy appeared and I noticed that he had a green sticker on his lapel with the words 'End H Block'. His father was civil and friendly, and reassured me that I was on the right road. A little further on I found that a road marked clearly on my map had ceased to exist. It had been blown up where it crossed the border and the bog was reclaiming it. The light was fading and Lough na Blaney Bane seemed lonely and melancholy. I was very relieved when I finally met Mrs McKenna, and she took me back to her warm and comfortable farm house.

Day 15   Wednesday 11 April:
to Caledon

Mrs McKenna kindly returned me to Lough na Blaney Bane in the morning, where I continued on the road towards Favor Royal Forest. The first section of this forest, at Altadeven, contains St Patrick's Chair and Well, which I went to inspect. I thought it one of the most attractive sites associated with St Patrick. The seat is a large block of mossy stone, and

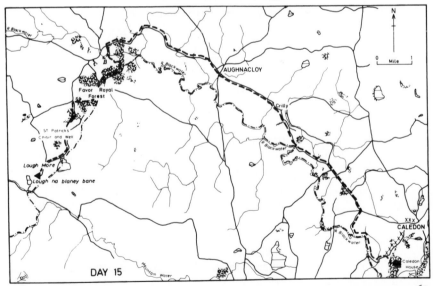

the well is a natural basin in the rock below, and all around is forest greenery. From here the pleasant forest road runs through a belt of very tall larch trees.

When I crossed the road into another section of Favor Royal Forest I had some trouble in finding a route, but eventually I passed the deserted 'Big House', set amid fine trees and parkland, and emerged on to the Aughnacloy road. It is hoped that the Way will eventually follow the Blackwater River, but I realised that an attempt to follow it now would slow me up considerably, and I had about nineteen miles to do. So I stuck to the road and reached Aughnacloy in time to go to the bank and buy some film. In the town a stranger greeted me and asked if I was the man walking the Ulster Way. He had heard of my venture on the radio. I was pleased by his friendly encouragement. It was now about lunch-time, so I decided to get a drink with my bread and cheese. I picked on the Dew Drop Inn, where I found an empty bar and was served by an elderly woman. I asked her if I might eat my lunch there. She invited me to come and eat it in her kitchen, where there was a fire, and where she was proposing to have her own lunch. So I got out my little lunch box and she helped herself to the fish and potatoes she had been cooking on her range. She was quite without self-consciousness or any embarrassment at lunching with a stranger, as she ate her potatoes out of the pot (a sensible thing to do in a cold climate), and licked her fish plate clean. We chatted about travelling, and I learnt that she had been nine times on a pilgrimage to Lough Derg in Co. Donegal.

I soon took to the road again because I had an appointment with a television crew. I had agreed to meet Patrick Burns, of the BBC in Belfast, at Ramaket, on the road from Aughnacloy to Caledon. I was on the main road for a time, but I turned off it at Crilly, and took a minor road as far as Curlagh, where I rejoined the main road. This side-road took me through pleasant parkland (part of Crilly desmesne) and farm land with trees and a hamlet or two. It seemed like a quiet English landscape, utterly unlike the wild bog and moorland around Lough na Blaney Bane, where I had started to-day's walk. I was struck again with the astonishing variety of the Ulster landscape.

I met the television crew on the main road not far from Ramaket. This was a particularly dull stretch of main road, so we moved for the filming off the road into a little wood where there was a convenient track. I had never been televised before so I was curious to see what would happen. It was very simple. I was asked to walk along the track, first by myself, and then talking to Patrick Burns.

At Ramaket I turned off the main road and took a small lane leading me down towards the Blackwater River. The lane petered out but I went on through fields to the bank of the river, a pleasant winding slow-moving stream with willows growing on the banks. I followed the river down to Anaghroe bridge, on the border of Co. Monaghan. The bridge has been mostly destroyed and can no longer be used by cars, but I was able to cross it and set foot in Co. Monaghan. I turned away from the river and followed the road to the entrance to Caledon estate. I entered the massive gates and followed a long drive through a fine stretch of park and woodland. I saw plenty of game—pheasants, mallard, rabbits— and in the distance I could hear the crying of peacocks. I walked up to Caledon Castle, curious to see what it would be like. I was somewhat taken aback to find myself confronted with a barbed wire fence, and behind it was a large Alsatian dog barking menacingly. It must be remembered that this estate is right up against the border in South Tyrone, and security precautions are essential. I rang the bell at the perimeter of the enclosure, and Lord Caledon came out to bring me in, first putting the Alsatian on a lead, much to my relief. We then entered the fine

Not far away, at Tynan Abbey, Sir Norman Stronge and his son were murdered in 1981, and their house burnt to the ground.

Georgian House through an imposing pillared portico. The Castle, which is not a fortified building, but a large dwelling house or mansion, was built by Thomas Cooley in 1779 and a colonnade by Nash was added in 1812. The outside is impressive, but the inside is beautifully proportioned, both elegant and spacious. I was shown to a room on the first floor, the finest bedroom I have ever slept in. My bed was a magnificent four-poster, in white and gold. Behind sliding white doors was a concealed washbasin, and a cupboard; and in a little room off the entrance was a private lavatory. The large room was clearly centrally heated, so that I had all the modern conveniences in a room that had lost none of its fine Georgian qualities of lofty elegance.

I had a hot bath and dried myself on an enormous white bath towel that matched the proportions of the house. Then I came down to one of the smaller, snugger rooms (if one can use the word 'snug' of a Georgian room) where I was offered a welcome whisky and soda. Dinner was a leisurely, pleasant meal, served in the very spacious, modernised kitchen. We had consommé, followed by a quiche, with a green salad and an excellent bottle of white wine, then Stilton and coffee. I could not help contrasting this kitchen with the one in the Dew Drop Inn, where I had lunched. I count myself lucky to have experienced such contrasts, and to have seen so many different interiors on this pilgrimage of mine.

In the course of conversation I discovered that Lady Caledon was deaf in the right ear, and that her daughter was deaf in the left. This gave us something in common, because I am deaf in one ear also. They were both going to fly to London in the morning to see a specialist. This meant an early breakfast, which suited me very well, so I retired to my beautiful Georgian four-poster and slept a blissful sleep.

Day 16   Thursday 12 April:
to Drumlee

In the morning I was almost lost in Caledon Castle. I knew that breakfast was being served in the kitchen, but I couldn't find the kitchen. I came down the stairs into the most beautiful octagon hall with four doors opening off it, but none of them seemed to lead to the kitchen. I couldn't recall exactly how we had got to it last night. I went towards the front of the house and went back upstairs, but I could find no one about to ask. For a few moments I was really

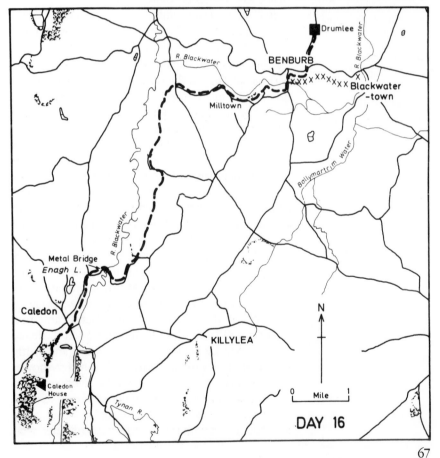

nonplussed. I seriously considered blowing my whistle for help. Then at last I hit on the right passage and found my way to breakfast.

After breakfast I walked from the Castle down the main avenue to the lodge gates. In the spacious rolling parkland there were some fine old trees. I saw more pheasants, and also a group of deer in the distance. There is a herd of 150 red deer on the estate. As I was walking into Caledon village, I was again offered a lift, which I had to decline. Then I was approached by two free-lance reporters, who took a few notes, and then some television shots. I never saw the end result of this.

In Caledon I was reminded of the 'troubles'. A fire bomb had been thrown at the Northern Bank building the previous night, and as I passed it I saw the blackened walls and windows. Caledon village was mostly built at the same time as the Castle, and it has a fine main street of Georgian stone buildings, including a market—house and courthouse. But I soon turned down towards the river, which I was hoping to follow. The shortest approach to it seemed to be past the local sewage works. A gate at the entrance was locked, so I climbed over it. As I did so I thought I heard someone shout 'Hey!' Because I hear with only one ear, I find it hard to tell the direction of a shout. I looked all around me but could see no one, so I went on, and nothing more happened. On the whole of my long journey this was the nearest I ever came to encountering any opposition to my progress. At first it was fairly easy to follow the bank of the river Blackwater, though it was very muddy going in places. Then I came to a really formidable double fence, which I finally surmounted by taking off my rucksack and partly climbing an overhanging tree. As a heavy shower was approaching I moved from the river bank to a minor road running nearby, where there was a farm. I had my elevenses in a pleasant dry hay-barn, and I also had a chat with the friendly young farmer, who

As the map indicates the S.C. route follows the boundary of the Caledon Castle estate round into Caledon village. For security reasons it is not possible to establish a public way through the estate. It is possible however, for individuals to obtain permission to pass through the estate by writing beforehand to Caledon Estates Office, Caledon, Co. Tyrone.

had been a student at UCD and had hitch-hiked in the USA.

I followed the road to an old metal bridge over the river. This was in a sad state of disrepair, but I managed to cross it, and then I went in search of the old canal running parallel to the Blackwater. This was marked by a firm blue line on my map, but I soon discovered that it no longer exists. Most of it has been filled in, and there are several old canal bridges now suspended above dry land. Here and there is a weedy stretch of water still surviving. I followed the general line of the old canal, with some difficulty, as far as Collins bridge, and then took to the road again through Wilsonstown Upper, Tullymore and Milltown. At Milltown there was an old linen factory, which seemed to be still working (Joseph Orr, Milltown Ltd.) From this point I took a

The Blackwater River near Benburb

towpath between the river and the old canal, an attractive path with fine views of the Blackwater, which is more turbulent at this point, and has two weirs. On the path I met two girls out walking with a dog. These were the only walkers or ramblers that I had passed since leaving Portstewart more than a fortnight ago. The towpath brought me to Benburb (where long ago Owen Roe O'Neill defeated General Munro in the famous battle of the Yellow Ford) and here I crossed a footbridge to the north bank and then proceeded via Maydown bridge to Drumlee, where I had booked in at a small guest house.

Day 17   Friday 13 April: to Columbcille

I wanted stamps this morning to post a letter, so I walked into Blackwatertown. For some reason the Post Office was shut but an obliging man in the

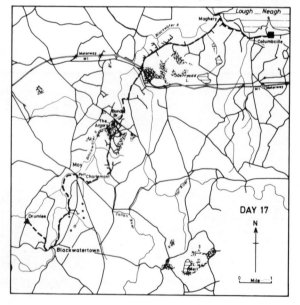

shop next door produced some stamps for me from his pocket. I then turned up a small byroad, still following the Blackwater. Just before I turned I was offered a lift by a police car. I declined, but I took the opportunity to ask them to convey a message to Sgt Ken McClean. When I had phoned him in Belfast the previous evening, I had been unable to get through.

After a mile or two following the lane, I tried walking along the river bank again. The river here flowed quietly and evenly, with salleys and willow trees growing on its banks. For a time I found stiles crossing the wire fences, presumably made to accommodate the fishermen who walked along the banks. But after a time these ceased, and I had to contend with fences and also with several dykes and ditches. As I approached the bridge between Moy and Charlemont I met one broad dyke that nearly defeated me. I felt fairly confident that I could jump it if I took a run, but not with a rucksack on my back. The difficulty was to throw the rucksack over and land it in a safe position, so that it would not roll back down the sloping bank into the water. I finally took a swing and let it go. It stayed put—just, and I was able to jump over and join it.

At Charlemont I took to the roads for a time, because I knew that there was no way to cross the Callan river, which flows into the Blackwater, except by the road bridge. But I turned back to the river bank at the Argory estate, one of the loveliest stretches of the Blackwater. I had previously explored with delight and curiosity this seemingly deserted but lovely demesne with Georgian buildings and tree-lined walks. It was at snowdrop time that I had first seen it, and there was one most beautiful avenue of pollarded lime trees with banks of snowdrops lining it from end to end. Now the snowdrops had gone, but the avenue was still lovely. I saw a blue jay amongst the trees of the estate, and on the river alongside it I saw the blue flash of a kingfisher crossing the water.

The Argory estate belonged to Sir Walter Bond, who apparently lived mostly in the south of France. He died recently and in 1981 the estate was presented to the National Trust by his son, Mr W. A. N. McGeogh Bond. It is now open to the public but the restoration work is still proceeding.

71

After Bond's Bridge it became increasingly difficult to follow the river bank, so I left it and took to the road for Maghery. As I was passing an apple orchard a farmer stepped out and greeted me. He seemed to know who I was and what I was doing. He turned out to be Hugh Vallely, the Chairman of the local Sports Council and an enthusiast for the Ulster Way project. His unexpected friendly greeting was a great encouragement to me on a rather dull stretch of the road.

I passed a bombed and deserted hotel at Maghery, and went on to Columbcille, getting pleasant vistas of Lough Neagh to the north. At Columbcille a young couple, Francis and Margaret Campbell, had kindly agreed to take me in for the night, and they gave me a warm and friendly welcome.

Day 18   Saturday 14 April: to Poyntzpass

The Ulster Way is designed to follow the course of the river Bann, which runs into Lough Neagh at Bannmouth, up through Portadown, and then to pick up the towpath on the old Newry Canal and follow it to Newry. I was only about a mile from Bannmouth and here there was a hand-operated ferry which would take me across to the east bank, which I had been told was the best side for walking. All I had to do was to get to the bank of the river and shout for the ferryman. I set off early after a good night's sleep, but when I got to the ferry there was no sign of life. I shouted, and then blew my whistle. Eventually a man appeared at the opposite side and shouted over to me that the ferry service was not operating, because the ferryman was ill. I learnt later that the old ferryman had had a stroke. So I had to change my route and stay on the west bank. This

The ferry is unfortunately now permanently closed, so the S.C. route follows the minor roads on the West side of the river.

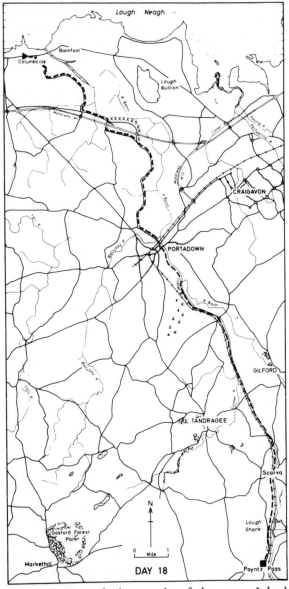

DAY 18

involved some further study of the map. I had already folded it and put it in my plastic map case. I had to take it out and refold it to show a different section. This sounds simple, but it was now raining and the wind was blowing, so I knocked again at the nearest door. It was a cottage where an old man lived alone. He invited me in with great courtesy, and I was able to fold my map in front of his pleasant turf fire.

He told me that it was very difficult to follow the west bank of the river Bann to Portadown, so I decided that it would be wise to stick to the byroads. I was disappointed at not being able to cross the river, but there was nothing I could do about it, so I set off down the road towards Portadown.

As I passed a farm I noticed that there were boxes of apples piled up in the yard. I had already seen these in one or two other farms and I was puzzled about the appearance of apples in April. There was a farmer in the yard, so I went in and asked him what he was doing with apples at this time of year. He told me that they were rejects from last season, now being brought out of store to be sent away to make apple juice.

The river was still not far away, so I asked this farmer if there was any possibility of crossing it somewhere. He told me that there was a chance that I might get a boat across at a house further down the road. But when I came to this house there was no sign of life anywhere. I knocked at the door twice, but nothing stirred, so I finally gave up all thoughts of crossing the river, and marched on down the road.

When I was passing another farm I saw a farmer with a bucket of water and a cloth. This gave me an idea. I was wearing my yellow waterproof over-trousers because it had been raining off and on. So I walked into the yard and asked the farmer if I might borrow his bucket and cloth to wipe down my trousers. He readily agreed, first filling me a fresh bucket of water. I sluiced down my trousers, and then walked on for them to dry in the wind.

I was approaching the M1, which I had to cross on my way to Portadown, and I could already hear the roar of traffic. In Crabtreelane I found a telephone kiosk and telephoned Nigel Jess of the N.I. Tourist Board, who had talked of meeting me in Portadown. I hardly knew Portadown, but he arranged to meet me at a grocery and home bakery belonging to one of his relatives. So I crossed over the motorway and pushed on for Portadown, along a rather dull road. The route from Bannmouth to Portadown had proved a rather unrewarding stretch of the Ulster Way, but just as I was entering the town a small incident occurred that cheered me on my way. A car with two girls in it stopped close to me. One of the girls got out and came to speak to me. She said that they had passed me on the road earlier, and she invited me to come and have lunch with them. I was delighted to be asked to lunch by two pretty girls, who were total strangers, but alas I had to refuse, since I was already committed to Nigel Jess. However they gave me a lift to the bakery where I was meeting him, and I was able to chat to them a little. It turned out that they were keen on walking. I made a note of their names—Clare and Ellie Donnelly—and if ever they should read this diary I would like them to know how much I appreciated their kindness, which helped to change my dull morning into an interesting day.

I joined Nigel for lunch on the west bank of the Bann where an English team of fishermen were practicing for the next day's international competition, between England, France and Ireland. These skilled professionals seemed to be pulling fish out of the river every few seconds. I had never seen anything like it. I was told that the fish, mostly roach, were kept in the storage nets to be weighed and counted and then were returned to the river. This seemed rather strange to me. As a not very skilful angler for small brown trout, I am always glad to take home my day's catch to be eaten.

After lunch Nigel accompanied me on my way southwards along the river path for about a mile.

The canal was built between 1731 and 1742 so that coal could be transported by water from Coalisland, on the shore of Lough Neagh, all the way to Dublin by water.

Then he had to return to look after the fishermen. I had taken the chance of his car to lighten my rucksack, and he had promised to drop my belongings at Mrs McComb's Guest House in Poyntzpass, which was my ultimate destination to-day. Unfortunately I had not realised soon enough that I was coming to the end of the map I was using, and I let go the one that I needed for the end of the day. At this point the Ulster Way is intended to follow the towpath of the old Newry canal, running from Newry to Portadown. It sounds simple enough to follow the line of an old canal, and I had thought that this would be an easy stretch of the Way for me, but it turned out to be more complicated than I had expected. At first the going was easy, a good hard path along the Bann from Portadown, and then the grassy bank of the Cusher river. But when I reached the bridge carrying the road from Lurgan and Waringstown to Tandragee (grid ref. 039508) I discovered that there were three separate channels of water, and I didn't know which one to follow and had no map to help me. I asked a motorist on the bridge and he advised the middle channel, which turned out to be right. Later on I went astray, following the Cusher river, but picked up the canal again later. Near Scarva the going got more difficult. The day had now warmed up and I was weary. I realised that there was likely to be an inn in Scarva and I was tempted by the thought of a pint of beer. So I went into the Commercial Inn and ordered a pint. This was all I wanted, but I got into conversation with the pople in the Inn, who were very friendly, and before I had drunk half my pint, another pint appeared alongside it, bought for me by Joe Moore. It seemed churlish to decline it, but I was a little worried. This was not the way to finish a long day's walk.

It turned out that Joe Moore and the proprietor of the Inn, Denis McCartney, were members of the Newry Canal Preservation Society, and they were delighted to meet someone who was walking along its banks. Joe showed me a dissertation on the canal, arguing for its preservation, and later on he kindly posted me a copy.

As soon as I decently could I left the inn and hastened on my way to Poyntzpass. Following the towpath proved difficult. At one point there was a formidable wire fence cutting right across it. In trying to climb it I balanced myself by getting my foot on a heap of dry sticks on the far side. A stick broke under me, and I was fairly caught with the top strand of barbed wire under the fork of my breeches. It took me some time and patience to disengage myself. Later on, the path was badly overgrown with brambles and churned up by the feet of many cattle. But soon the going improved, and I reached Poyntz-pass about 7.30 to find a small group of friendly local people waiting to welcome me, including my host. Mr and Mrs McComb were extremely kind and hospitable, and gave me VIP treatment. But I went to bed early, feeling very tired and also somewhat worried about the next two days ahead of me. I had miscalculated this section of the Ulster Way, thinking it would be easy going, because there were no hills or forests, and I had the canal to follow. So I had planned two long days, about 20 miles each, from Lough Neagh to Rostrevor, and then on the third day I would be crossing the Mournes to Newcastle on a route I didn't know, which was likely to involve some rough going.

I had miscalculated in another way, too. I had the mistaken notion that if I survived the first week of walking, I would be so fit that the rest would be easier, and I had not allowed myself a single rest-day in the whole schedule. This was a serious weakness in my planning, not so much because I needed a day's rest, though this would have been a good idea, but because it left no slack at all in my total plan. I had to reach a particular point every night. So now I had to resort to a small piece of cheating, in order to create a little slack for myself and give me more

Poyntzpass is a village at the highest point of the Newry canal. Road, railway and canal run side by side through the pass. There were ten locks lifting the canal up from Newry and five more dropping it down to Lough Neagh.

confidence about crossing the Mournes. I decided to follow the canal to Newry, taking it easily, and then to get on a bus, if I could find one, from Newry to Rostrevor.

Day 19   Easter Sunday, 15 April: to Rostrevor

I had a slight headache this morning, and I still felt a little daunted by the prospects ahead of me, but it was a beautiful sunny morning, and when I got into my stride along the canal I began to feel better. I fell in with a farmer who was going my way for a time, and we talked of the weather and birds. I had seen what I thought was a swallow, and there were swans nesting on the old canal.

Soon after I had reached Jerrets Pass I was met by Mrs Charlie Halliday, one of those in the group that had welcomed me to Poyntzpass the previous evening, and she invited me up to her house for a cup of tea. Since I was taking an easy day I was glad to accept and I spent a pleasant half-hour resting and chatting. Charlie Halliday had built his own house, and a tiny toy church alongside it.

The S.C. route from Newry to Rostrevor does not follow the shoreline of Carlingford Lough but goes inland over the hills, offering some fine views of the Mourne country-side. This first section of the Mourne Trail, which is intended to run as far as Newcastle, has been waymarked by the D.O.E. Roads Service. The first sign will be found in Abbey Yard and the trail goes out of Newry along Chapel Road. The waymarking is somewhat different from that used on other sections of the Ulster Way, consisting of small metal plaques.

Later on I had a prolonged and lazy lunch sprawled in the sun with my socks and shoes off. The going was mostly easy today, but I still encountered some bad patches of deep mud and thorn bushes, and at one point there was a complete blockage of the path, so that I had to leave the canal for a time and make a detour. I reached Newry in the afternoon and found that there was a convenient bus going to Rostrevor via Warrenpoint.

When I reached Rostrevor my next concern was to see if I could lighten my pack by sending on a parcel to the Guest House in Newcastle where I was to stay. There seemed little hope of getting it round by bus so I found a taxi-driver who agreed to take it.

78

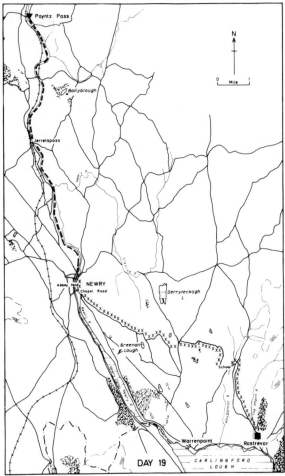

I gave him as much as I could, including my water-proof anorak and overtrousers, since the weather prospects were good. I even decided that I could sleep that night without pyjamas. So later I sat down to an excellent dinner with the hospitable Kennedys in my old knee-breeches and stockings. There was a bottle of wine in my honour which I much appreciated. So I went to bed well rested after an easy day and in good spirits for climbing the Mournes next day.

Day 20   Monday 16 April:
to Newcastle

Rostrevor is a small sheltered resort on Carlingford Lough, with a mild climate. There are several guest-houses here, and it makes a good base for the Mourne country.

Mrs Kennedy kindly laid on an early breakfast for me and I was able to leave the house at 8.00 on a fine morning. I walked northwards through Rostrevor Forest to the Yellow Water River, still in the shadow of the mountain. I found a very attractive mountain path, going up beside the river, crossing it at one point by a footbridge. The path was delightfully soft with pine-needles in places, kind to the sore toe that was still troubling me. When I emerged from the forest on to the open slopes of the mountains I was somewhat uncertain of my direction, but I caught a glimpse of Slieve Donard in the distance and this gave me a general line to aim at. I crossed the Hilltown–Kilkeel road near Pigeon Rock mountain, and went right past the source of the Bann, a delightful clear burn cascading down the mountain-side.

I had my lunch on the shoulder of Slieve Muck, and saw in the distance the first ramblers I had en-

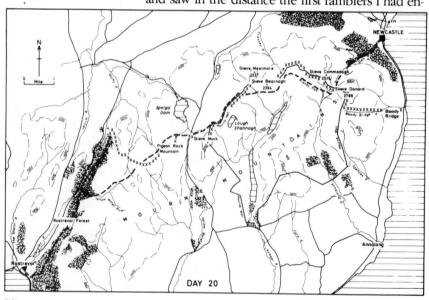

The Mourne Wall

There is now an excellent detailed large scale map (1:25,000, approx. 2½" to 1 mile) of the Mourne country, produced by the Ordnance Survey of Northern Ireland. The Ulster Way is marked on this map by a broken red line. There are two alternative routes diverging at Deers Meadow, south of the Spelga Dam. One route goes over the high peaks and follows a part of the Mourne Wall. The other route takes lower ground and goes further north, passing Fofanny Dam,

countered since leaving Portstewart. It was a fine Easter Monday and there were several groups of walkers in the hills. This was lucky for me, because I drifted too far south on the slopes of Meelbeg and Bearnagh, and might have missed the Hare's Gap if it had not been for a timely encounter with a lone rambler, who directed me towards it. From the Hare's gap I picked up the Brandy Pad, but left it shortly after The Castles to follow a small path up to the Wall again, over it and down the Glen River into Donard Park. I went this way because I knew it would bring me out close by Mrs Henderson's Guest House, where I was to stay the night.

I arrived on her door-step at 6.30, weary but happy that I had had a successful day, and ready for hot water, food and rest. But I was met by a girl who told me that Mrs Henderson was ill in hospital and

and going through Tolly-more Forest Park. It is this latter route that is way-marked and described in the Ulster Way leaflet 7A, Mourne Trail, Section 2.
The sketch-map for Day 20 (p. 80) shows only the high-level route.

Newcastle, which is the main seaside resort on the south Down coast, has several hotels and guest-houses. There is also a youth hostel in Downs Road (closed in January).

that there was no possibility of my staying in the house that night. She offered to take me in her car to find a hotel. I was glad to accept her offer and fortunately the parcel of my belongings that had been brought from Rostrevor was already there. So I got into her car, wondering what accommodation would be available in Newcastle on an Easter Monday night. I was lucky to get in almost immediately at the Brook Cottage Hotel, and my first thought was a hot bath. I shed my clothes and took a fine big white towel to the bathroom with me. But when I turned on the hot tap, no water came out of it. It had been such a busy day at the hotel that their water-tank was empty. So I had to content myself with a jug of hot water from the bar. I had a brief wash, and then a long drink of beer, and after that I did justice to the excellent fillet steak that was put before me.

Day 21 Tuesday 17 April: to Murphystown

The Murlough Nature Reserve is a National Trust reserve established on the sand-dunes south of Dundrum. It has a special badger gate.

I began my walk today along the wide flat shore of Newcastle Strand, and I was able to look back at the sweep of the Mournes behind me and feel that I was making progress on the long circle of the Ulster Way. I followed the strand to Murlough Nature Reserve. The sand eventually became very soft and hard to walk on with the weight of a rucksack sinking one's feet into it, so I entered the Nature Reserve, a truly delightful place, where I wished I could have lingered, but I passed on through a pleasant shady avenue and over a bridge into Dundrum, where I did a little shopping and made some phone calls. I went on, more or less following the shore line, using an old railway track for a time, and then going through Ballykinler towards Tyrella Sands. At times I was walking on the shore, but when it seemed too

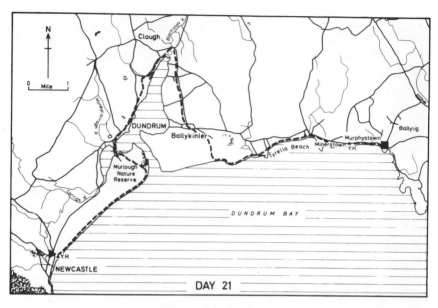

DAY 21

rough and rocky I turned up into fields and past houses. At one point some children called out to me, 'Hey mister what are you doing in our garden?' but they didn't seem to be hostile.

At Tyrella Sands I found myself on a beach resort in the midst of a holiday crowd, making the most of the fine weather. There were cars, people kicking balls, and even some hardy children bathing in the sea. To avoid wetting my feet by walking through the river at the end of the beach I turned up on to the coast road and stuck to this, in spite of fairly heavy holiday traffic, until I came to the turn to Ballylig where I was spending the night at Mrs McCordie's Farm Guest House.

My arrival at Ballylig House, a pleasing cluster of farm buildings amongst trees, was in sharp contrast with my arrival at the Brook Cottage Hotel last night. There it was all bustle and hassle, crowds in the bar, and a struggle to get some hot water. This is such a peaceful, quiet place, with lovely big rooms. I had a welcome bath, then a pot of tea in the living room, a gracious, spacious room with attractive period

The youth hostel at Minerstown, near Tyrella Sands, which is marked on most maps, is now closed.

83

Looking back at the Mournes from Dundrum Castle, on the route north from Newcastle

furniture and large sash windows. There were views out over wide stretches of country, away to the sea and the Mournes. Nearer at hand I could see horses and beech-trees with nesting rooks.

Day 22   Wednesday 18 April: to Portaferry

Bill Kirk, a photographer from the NI Tourist Board, came to the farm this morning to take some pictures of me, together with the farm dog and an attractive little foal. He gave me a lift back to the line of the Ulster Way, and I made my way to Killough, via St John's Point, following the general line of the coast, sometimes on the shore, sometimes in fields and

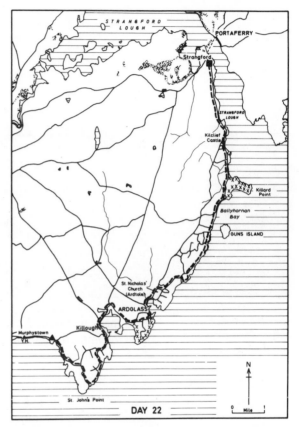

STRANGFORD
LOUGH

PORTAFERRY

Strangford

STRANGFORD
LOUGH

Kilclief
Castle

Killard
Point

Ballyhornan
Bay

GUNS ISLAND

St. Nicholas'
Church
(Ardtole)

ARDGLASS

Killough

Murphystown
Y.H.

St. John's Point

DAY 22

N

0   Mile   1

along the road. I passed St John's Church, which was built in the 10th century and is now just a small bare stone skeleton.

I followed the old railway track out of Killough until I had to turn aside at a broken bridge. Then I took the road, but I turned off it up a narrow little lane to find a quiet sunny spot to eat my lunch. Here I had one of my oddest and most amusing encounters. I had almost finished lunch and was stretched out on the bank of a ditch, with my boots off, when a farmer came down the lane in a small car. He stopped and, leaning out of the car, asked: 'Are you enjoying yourself?' I replied that I was indeed, and we began a conversation. When he

85

Approaching Portaferry by the ferry from Strangford.

heard that I had retired from the New University of Ulster, he immediately asked me the meaning of the word 'metempsychosis'. I managed to explain the word, somewhat hesitantly, and he went on to talk about philosophy and the immortality of the soul. From this he switched to literature and gave me quotations from Pope to complete, such as: 'A little learning is a dangerous thing,' and I chimed in with 'Drink deep, or taste not, the Pierian spring.' Then he began to sing Handel's setting of Pope's *Pastoral.* This is one of my favourite tunes and I was able to join him for a few lines. Then he went on to Tom Moore's 'Meeting of the Waters'. We parted on cordial terms, hoping that we might meet again. I learnt that he had been a student at Queen's University in Belfast and that his name was Crangel.

I went on my way, past Artole church, a medieval ruin on a most attractive raised site. Then I went down to the shore again and past St Patrick's Well, a disappointing concrete enclosure, not nearly as attractive as St Patrick's Chair and Well in Favor

The Ulster Way continues through Strangford and along the shoreline of Strangford Lough, but there was no accommodation available in Strangford, so it seemed sensible for me to cross by the ferry to the Portaferry Hotel.

Royal Forest. I passed Sheepland Harbour and then took a small winding coast road, which led me finally to a delightful cliff path on smooth green sward, above a rocky coastline. I followed this as far as Ballyhornan, then walked on the beach again for a time, but I cut across Killard Point and took the road to Kilclief Castle. From here I followed the main road to Strangford and then took the ferry across to the Portaferry Hotel, where I was booked in for the night.

Day 23   Thursday 19 April: to Killyleagh

One of the problems of staying in a hotel is the difficulty of getting off to an early start. When I went down to breakfast at 8.00 there was no sign of life

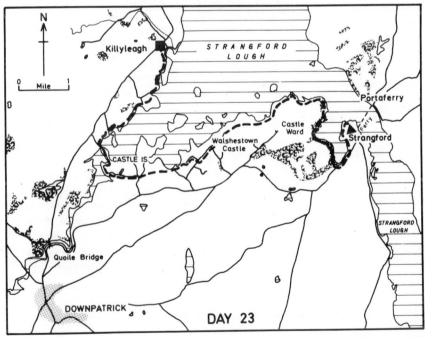

Strangford Castle is a sixteenth century tower house, one of several built by English settlers who established themselves strongly on the shores of Strangford Lough. There are four other castles nearby–Old Castle Ward, Audley's Castle, Walshestown Castle and Kilclief Castle.

Castle Ward, once the eighteenth century residence of Lord and Lady Bangor, is now a National Trust Property. It has some curious and interesting architectural features, and the attractive grounds contain a wildfowl lake.

anywhere in the hotel, but soon someone turned up from outside and began to get me some breakfast. My next problem was to recover some socks and handkerchiefs that I had given to Anne, one of the hotel staff, to be washed. Anne had not yet appeared, and I thought I might have to abandon them, but somebody found them in the tumble-drier, so I thrust them into my rucksack and set off for the ferry to Strangford. Wilfred and Evelyn Capper were waiting for me on the jetty. They gave me faithful support throughout my long walk, and I was to stay with them on my way through Hollywood later.

I soon set off on the next stage of the Way, following the east shoreline of Strangford Lough. I passed Strangford Castle and then was puzzled by being confronted by a private gate barring my way forward, but to the left of the gate I found the beginning of a small lane, and a notice reading: 'Squeeze Cut, leading to Strangford Bay Path.' This was a pleasant little lane, reminding me of those often found in English villages, and it led me to the helpfully signposted Strangford Bay Path, which I followed round to the main road. I soon turned off this at the entry to Castle Ward, and walked through the woods. I found a bird-watchers' hide at the edge of the water, called Eagleson's Hide (dedicated to the memory of Robert Eagleson, Vice-President of the Ulster Society for the Protection of Birds, 1957–60). It was raining gently, so I took my elevenses (a drink of hot coffee) in the hide, looking out at the birds. These were mostly swans, gulls and oyster-catchers. I had no time to wait for rarer species, so I pressed on round the bay until I came to the Wildfowl Sactuary at Temple Water. I went through the Sanctuary along a pleasant grassy route, passing groups of geese and children, coming out again past Audley's Castle, still following the path along the shore. The path petered out, but I continued to follow the shoreline as best I could. The shore was

The lake at Castle Ward

rough and slippery and for the first time since I had set out I lost my footing and fell. I fell awkwardly, cutting my left thumb and my right shin. There was a farmhouse on the hillside close by me, and I decided to seek help, out of the rain, to get my wounds washed and dressed. A woman opened the door for me and received me rather cautiously at first—I was certainly a very unusual caller—but civilly, and she showed me where I could wash. Gradually, as we talked, she became more friendly and relaxed. She gave me a seat by the fire and offered me tomato soup, which I gratefully accepted. Then she made me tea and gave me a generous tot of whisky. Meantime I had put on dry socks and was altogether in better shape to go on my way.

I cut across fields to the shore again, where the

going was not too bad, but there was no path to follow, and the shoreline was very irregular. So I went inland again past Walshestown Castle and later followed a minor road to Ringban, then down to the shore again; but I soon had to leave it and go across fields and over fences until I finally struck the road to Castle Island. This island is another bird sanctuary and I saw a great many water birds, such as duck, geese, grebes and coots. Inland I had a remarkably good view of a stoat, hunting along the banks of a ditch not far from the road.

I passed through the premises of Quoile Yacht Club and crossed the causeway. Near sluice gates I spoke to some workmen from the Department of Agriculture and they told me it was possible to follow the shoreline. So I tried it, but found the going increasingly difficult, over sloppy, slippery seaweed and sharp stones. I passed Mullough Bay and finally found a road near the shore, but here I took a wrong turn and found myself approaching a large house near Moore's Point. It was a most attractive house, beautifully situated with fine views out over the Lough. I decided to knock at the door and ask my way. I met with an immediate friendly reception. I was invited in, given the use of the telephone and then a large whisky and soda. Mrs Lindsay had seen me on the television screen and recognised me at once. I was seated in front of a big log fire, and so I ended this day in comfort and sociability. I was to meet Dick Rogers in Killyleagh, because he and his wife were putting me up for the night. At first I still intended to walk the remaining two miles into Killyleagh, but after my second glass of whisky my resolution weakened and I accepted Col. Lindsay's kind offer to take me there in his car. He took me to the Dunmore Hotel, where Dick Rogers met me and drove me to his house in Ballylighorn Road near Comber, where I spent a pleasant sociable evening and a comfortable night. Dick and his wife Kitty are lovers of country life and

country walks. Dick is the author of one of the Irish
Walk Guides. Kitty is something of a painter. I was
struck by one of her paintings, which faced me
across the dining-table—a haunting picture of
women's faces behind wire.

Day 24 Friday 20 April: to Newtownards

To-day I was lucky to have a guide and companion
most of the day. We all drove to Killyleagh Castle,
and then Dick walked with me northwards along the
route of the Ulster Way. We kept near to the shore of
Strangford Lough, but we were on tarred roads and
lanes all day, passing some interesting cottages and
houses. One of them was Toye House, an attractive
Georgian building with a spacious doorway.

I thought how different the Co. Down landscape
here was from some of the other parts of Ulster that
I had passed through, especially in the west. This was
rolling fertile country, civilised and inhabited for
centuries, with much arable land and many houses.
As we moved north, nearer to the larger towns, we
saw an increasing number of glossy villas and com-
muter houses. But this countryside is very attractive
in its own way, undulating and varied, with woodland and pasture and rolling ploughed fields, and
delightful vistas into the blue distances of the Lough.

We had lunch in a little side-lane near Seaview,
and a young man from a nearby house approached
us. He had seen me on TV and recognised me as we
passed. He was very friendly and offered us tea or
the use of his telephone. We went into his house and
chatted for a short time. Soon after, as we were
passing through Ballydrain, I was amused and
pleased when two little girls ran out into the road
and asked me for my autograph.

At Castle Espie we turned again towards Dick's

91

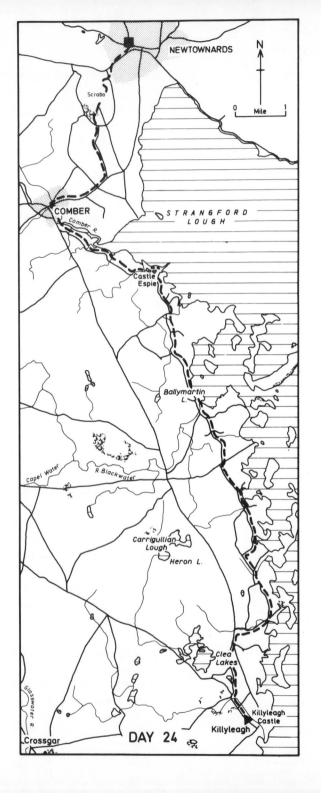

house, where Kitty received us with welcome tea and cake. Then Dick drove me through Comber in the Newtownards direction, and I took to the road again, heading for the Scrabo Tower. I went through the Scrabo Country Park, climbing up through large beech trees. At the top I should have followed the path round to the right, but I went straight on over the Golf Course, heading for the tower. The tower is a gaunt, stark Victorian column of brick, but it makes a fine landmark, and from it I had views back to the Mournes and on over Belfast.

I took a steep track down the hill and walked into Newtownards, where I was to spend a pleasant and comfortable night at the Guest House run by Mrs Crosbie Cochrane, wife of the gardening expert frequently heard on radio.

Day 25   Saturday 21 April: to Hollywood

Wilfrid Capper called for me this morning at 9.00. He was to have accompanied me on today's lap, but he had pulled a muscle in his leg, jumping over a stream in Donegal, so he was only able to walk a little way with me, to show me the direction out of Newtownards. I headed north towards Helen's Tower. This prominent feature made it easy for me to find my way while I was on the open hillside, but once I entered the forest I could no longer see the Tower. I took a wrong turning somewhere and drifted west, so that I never actually passed the Tower. I was aiming for the George Inn, where I knew that Major Jock Affleck, the Recreation Officer of the Bangor Borough Council, would be waiting for me. But I eventually emerged from the forest on to the road about a mile away from the George. Wilfrid Capper came to my rescue in his car and brought me to the meeting point.

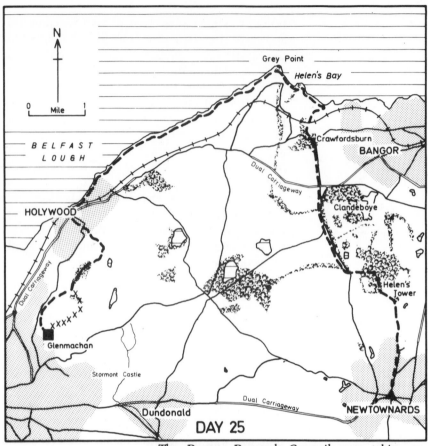

DAY 25

The Bangor Borough Council were taking an
interest in the Ulster Way and they had arranged a
small informal reception for me. Soon the Mayor
arrived, Mrs Mary O'Fee, and we all went for coffee
in the Mayor's Parlour at Bangor Town Hall. When I
began my walk I never expected to set foot in any
Town Hall, but I enjoyed this pleasant informal
occasion. While I was drinking my coffee out of an
elegant cup in these dignified surroundings, I
recalled my usual elevenses from a flask and plastic
mug, in a hay-barn or on a hillside. After coffee I was
interviewed by the editor of the *Bangor Spectator*
who took some photographs and asked me

questions about my journey. Then we returned to the George, and the Mayor and Major Affleck walked with me to Crawfordsburn Glen. Here Wilfrid joined us again and we went on to Helen's Bay. I took leave of my companions here and went on alone along the coastal path towards Holywood. This was a pleasant path with open views across Belfast Lough towards Carrickfergus. It was mostly a properly constructed path, though in places one just followed the beach.

To-day's route was all entirely new to me, and my next problem was to find my way through Holywood. I was told to look for the maypole, but I didn't at first recognise the maypole, which seemed to me more like a ship's mast than the maypoles I remembered from my boyhood on the village green at Ilmington in Warwickshire. However, I finally picked up the trail through Holywood and on to the hills above where I found the Nun's Walk. But then I lost the trail again and came down on to the old Holywood Road, instead of going on to the junction of Glenmachen Road and Belmont Road where Wilfrid had arranged to meet me, because I was staying the night with him.

This seems to have been my day for lost meeting points. Wilfrid and I had different maps, and when we agreed on a meeting place, there must have been some misunderstanding. This would not have mattered if I had kept on the right trail, because I would have come to the junction where he was waiting for me. Instead I made my way to the junction of the old Holywood Road with Quarry Road, and waited there patiently for a long time. Then I realised something must be wrong. I walked on to the next junction. No sign of Wilfrid. I knocked on the door of the nearest house and asked if I might use the telephone. I telephoned Mrs Capper to find that Wilfrid had not yet returned. I walked back to my first point, but there was still no sign of Wilfrid. What should I do? I decided to phone for a taxi, and

I knocked on the door at 51 Quarry Road. Once more I was lucky to find a good samaritan who came to my rescue. Instead of letting me phone for a taxi, Mr Haig got out his own car and drove me to Wilfrid's home at Carney Hill. Wilfrid was still out, waiting patiently for me at the junction. But eventually he came home too. After all this it was not surprising that the dinner that Evelyn had prepared for us some three hours before had considerably cooled off.

Day 26   Sunday 22 April: to Dunmurry

This was my dullest day, mostly through suburban streets from Glenmachen to Belvoir Park. I was on

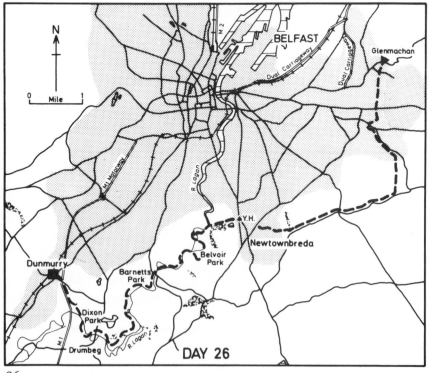

tarred roads the whole way, but my walk was occasionally enlivened by people recognising me, and giving me encouraging greetings.

The Belfast Youth Hostel is near Belvoir Park, at 11 Saintfield Road. It is open from 1 January to 21 December.

I had explored Belvoir Park previously so I was able to find the route without difficulty, and the path along the Lagan River is a pleasant one, but it soon began to rain heavily and I had a wet and weary trudge along the river path to Drumbeg bridge. There is a pleasant little country church here, with yew-tree arches, and three of my cousins lie buried there. I sheltered for a short while under the roof of the lych-gate at the church entrance, but then I went on through Dixon park to Dunmurry. This was the end of my stint for the day, and I thankfully climbed on to a bus into Belfast where I was spending the night with friends.

Day 27   Monday 23 April:
to Cavehill

The Ulster Way makes a loop around the south of Belfast and then climbs on to the hills to the west, going up Black Mountain and coming down from Cave Hill to cross the Antrim Road and the M2. I went back to Dunmurry to pick up the trail and headed westwards from Dunmurry station towards Colin Glen. The Way should have followed a stream and a thin green tongue of woodland, but this was blocked by dumps of rubble so I had to go up Suffolk Road. This seemed a squalid edge of Belfast, and there was much litter and wreckage. There were slogans and graffiti scrawled on the blank gable walls of a gaunt housing estate. Some were political—JOIN PROVOS—others personal perhaps. ARDER EASTY—what could that mean? I knew this was a Republican area, so I was a little apprehensive and thought it wiser not to take photographs. A police patrol passed me and later an Army Saracen. I

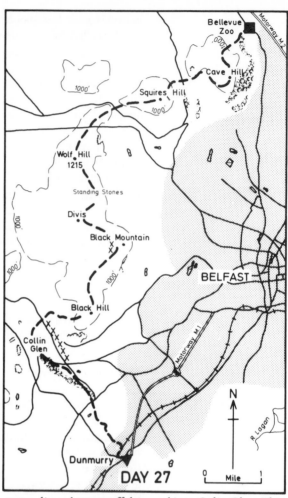

DAY 27

was relieved to get off the road into Colin Glen. This Glen is a National Trust property, but the sign had disappeared and the place had an abandoned, neglected air.

Much later, the murdered body of Dr Neidermeyer, the former German consul, was unearthed near here. I'm glad I didn't know the body was lying there when I passed.

After surmounting a very formidable wire fence at the side of the Glen I headed up past the Glenside Inn to the top of Black Mountain. From here I crossed a good deal of rough and boggy ground towards Divis Mountain, where I finally hit a tarred road called Walter's Way. Later a sign informed me that this road had been constructed by 33 Field Squadron, RE, between 25 July, 1974 and 18 October, 1974. From Divis I descended over boggy rough ground again towards Wolf Hill. I met a lad with three dogs, looking for hares. Apart from the soldiers guarding the radio station, he was the first person I had seen on these hills. With the large city of Belfast lying just below the hills it seemed strange that they should be so desolate and deserted. I thought of the hills above Sheffield and how many people I had encountered while walking there, even on weekdays. At the Cave Hill end, where the going is easier, and there are marked paths, I did see more people about.

I had my lunch by the broken wall of an old cottage. I noticed traces of lazy beds near by, where clearly potatoes had once been grown. At one time there were people living up here. Now there were only larks, hawks, pee-wits, hares and a few cows. After yesterday's dismal rain I found this a good day for walking. There were showers, and the wind was cold up on the hills, but there were bright sunny intervals and visibility was good, so that I could see my way ahead.

I went down through some abandoned gravel pits, crossed several roads and then climbed Squires Hill, and thence on to Cave Hill, where I followed a good path, with views over the city below, to McArt's Fort. I took a precipitous path down to the edge of the Zoo, and finally emerged on the Antrim Road. Here I took a bus again and returned to my friends, Cyril and Felicity Ehrlich, where I spent another pleasant, relaxed evening.

Day 28 Tuesday 24 April: to Ballyboley Forest

I returned to the Antrim Road below Cave Hill to do the next leg of the Way northwards towards the An-

99

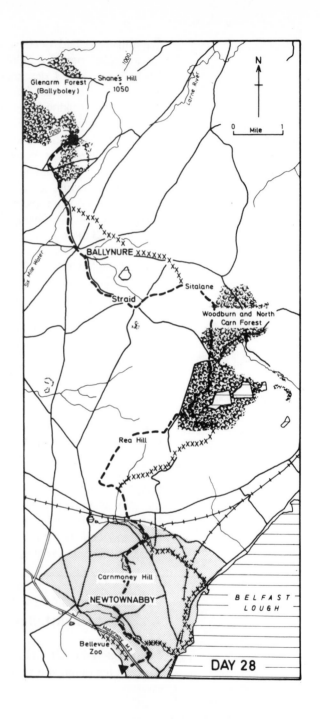

It was not possible to
establish a right of way
over private land on
Carnmoney Hill, so the
route has been altered
(see map for Day 28).
The trail through
Woodburn Forest has
now been waymarked.

trim Hills. I went over Carnmoney Hill and headed
for Woodburn Forest. It was a pleasant route through
this forest, with some open vistas and some decidu-
ous trees, as well as the ubiquitous spruce and pine
that can give a claustrophobic prison-house effect to
forest roads when they are unrelieved.

From Woodburn Forest I crossed the road into
North Carn Forest and here the track I was following
finally petered out altogether and left me to fight my
way through a dense patch of furze.

I eventually emerged on to a road that led me
towards Sitalane. There should have been a path
here leading off in a north–westerly direction, but I
never found it. I called at a farm nearby, partly in the
hope that the farmer would allow me to cut across
his land. He and his wife were both very welcoming
and friendly, but he directed me to take the road
through Straid and Ballynure, which I did, though it
was somewhat off the direct line of my route to
Ballyboley Forest. The entrance to this forest was
my objective for the day, and I reached it about five
o'clock. But I still had about five miles to go to get
to my night's lodging at the Kilwaughter House
Hotel, on the Larne side of Shane's Hill.

I was planning to hitch-hike this stretch, if I
possibly could. On the byroad leading up towards
Shane's Hill there was no traffic, so I had to walk it,
feeling a little resentful, because it was not part of
the Ulster Way. But as soon as I got on to the main
road I was lucky enough to get an immediate lift.
Squadron Leader Jimmy Speers and his wife
stopped for me. Air force personnel are not sup-
posed to give lifts to people in Ireland for security
reasons, but fortunately Mrs Speers recognised me. I
had walked nearly twenty miles when I got this
welcome lift, which saved me a weary trudge along
the main road, so my spirits were lifted as well as my
body. And when I got into the hotel I found an unexpected telegram from the East Antrim Ramblers,
sent by Hugh Munnis. It read: 'Keep right on to the

101

end of the road. Best wishes.' This, too, lifted my spirits, and I went to bed in a cheerful mood and slept like a log.

Day 29   Wednesday 25 April: to Glenarm

It is always difficult to get away early from a hotel but I managed to get some breakfast eventually, and I was out on the road soon after nine. Now I had the problem of getting back to Ballyboley Forest to pick up my trail. I stood for a time thumbing a lift, but no car stopped. I walked on past a bad bend in the road to reach a point where I thought I might be more successful. Here I tried again, but still there was no response. I debated with myself whether it was better to wait and keep trying, or whether I should walk on. If I had to walk in the end, then it was better to get moving. Just as I had decided to move, I saw another car coming, and I raised my thumb again. The driver stopped; he, too, had seen me on television and recognised me. That television interview, which I never saw myself, has been a great help to me.

The driver dropped me at the turn-off on Shane's Hill, and a woman at once approached me. She asked me to tell the farmer down the road that his lambs were out. I delivered the message and walked on to the entrance to the forest. Here I was able to check my route with a Forest Officer, and then I went on along a pleasant forest road, crossed the main road again and headed for Agnew's Hill. Here I had fine open views. To the east I looked out over Larne and Islandmagee, and to the south I could still see the Mournes. It was a fine bright day for the hills, but the strong north–west wind was cold on my head and face. I pulled the hood of my anorak over my cap to keep my ears warm.

Going down from Agnew's Hill I headed for Sallagh Braes, pausing on the way to look at a fine standing

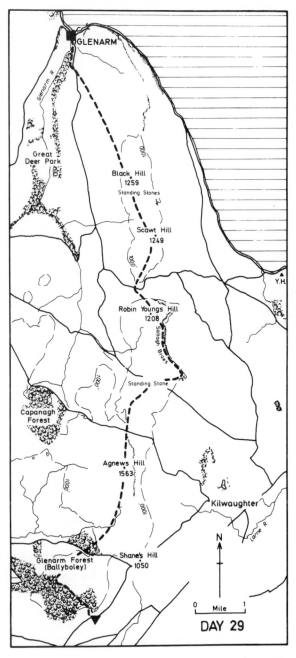

GLENARM

Glenarm R

Great
Deer Park

Black Hill
1259
Standing Stones

Scawt Hill
1249

1000

Y.H.

Robin Youngs Hill
1208

Slatagh Braes

Standing Stone

Capanagh
Forest

Agnews Hill
1563

Kilwaughter

Larne R

1000

N

Shane's Hill
1050

Glenarm Forest
(Ballyboley)

0   Mile   1

DAY 29

stone in a commanding position. Sallagh Braes is marked on the new O.S. map as a beauty spot, and rightly so. It is a beautiful natural amphitheatre of steep cliffs, affording fine sweeping views over the landscape below, with the sea about three miles away. The cliffs provide nesting places for many birds. I saw ravens and buzzards and jackdaws. The path follows the top of the curving line of cliffs, and in the bright spring sunshine I saw the Braes at their best. Leaving them reluctantly I cut over the shoulder of Robin Young's Hill towards Scawt Hill, Bally-gilbert Hill and Black Hill. The Way runs along this line of hills towards Glenarm. In fact, I kept below the crests to get a rest from the strong wind, and I headed as straight as I could for Glenarm.

I am now writing this in Margaret's Café in the main street in Glenarm. This is more café than guest house, but they do have beds, and I could find no-where else in Glenarm. I am writing at the table in a kind of back parlour, where I have just finished my tea. It is a curiously public place, rather like the waiting room of a small railway station. There is a big open fire and two old ladies are sitting beside it, one quietly belching. People keep coming and going through the room, some of them carrying Bibles. There seems to be some sort of revivalist meeting in prospect. I notice pious texts on the walls. One of them reads as follows:

Christ is the Head of this House
The Unseen Guest at every Meal
The Silent Listener to every conversation

Glenarm is the oldest of the villages in the Glens of Antrim. Glenarm Castle is the home of the Earl of Antrim, but a part of the desmesne has now become Glenarm Forest Park. The Castle re-sembles the Tower of London and Sandford (see bibliography) has an informative and amusing note on the entrance to it.

Day 30   Thursday 26 April:
to Cushendun

My bed last night had something of a sag in it, a thing that never agrees with me. I tried to sleep across it, and I did sleep, though it was not one of

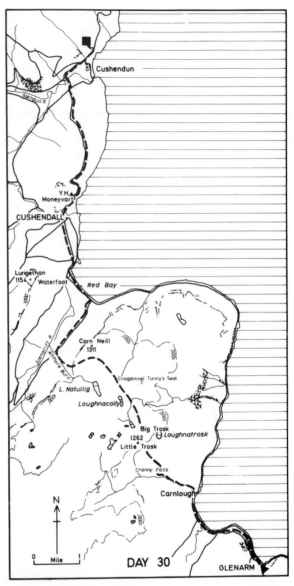

my best nights. But I had a good breakfast—porridge followed by a fry—and Mrs Morrow, the proprietress, only charged me £4 for supper, bed and breakfast, which was remarkably cheap.

The weather was good for walking, sunny and dry, and the weather forecast held a promise that the cold northerly winds would moderate. I was now on a stretch of the Way that I had not explored at all previously, though I had the benefit of the new O.S. map. At first it was simple. From Glenarm I followed the coast round Straidkilly Point, taking the minor road above the A2 (the main coast road). At Glencloy I joined the main road for a time, then walked on the beach to Carnlough. At Carnlough I had to climb inland, over the boggy plateau towards Glenariff. I knew I had to steer between Little Trosk and Big Trosk, and I was anxious to check that I was heading for the right peaks. I asked one or two local people but they seemed never to have heard of Big or Little Trosk. Finally, as I walked up the road towards the Cranny Falls, I met a man on a tractor who gave me some help. He confirmed my identification of the Trosks, and advised me not to take the route past the Cranny Falls. Although the Way is intended to take in these falls, marked on the map as a beauty spot, I accepted this local man's advice because I knew I had a long day ahead of me.

In spite of the cold wind I noticed spring flowers everywhere in evidence. To-day I have seen primroses, violets, wood-anemones, celandines and dandelions—and even a few clumps of daffodils. But soon I was above the level of most wild flowers, and aware only of the silence of the hills. From the shoulder of Little Trosk, I was heading for Lough Natullig, and beyond that for the Altmore Burn, which falls down a gully into the Glenariff valley. But I could not see Lough Natullig, and even though I took a compass bearing to start me off in the right direction I eventually drifted north, and found myself heading for Carn Neill. I then turned west towards Altmore Burn, but I never saw Lough Natullig until it was well behind me. It often happens that a feature like this, so large and unmistakable on the map, proves difficult to locate on the ground.

One mile north of Cushendall there is the youth hostel at Moneyvart (closed in December).

I followed Altmore Burn down to the road below, and then took this road to Red Bay. Here I went on to the beach and walked barefooted for a time, to rest my feet and bathe my sore toe in sea-water. I walked on through Waterfoot and Cushendall to Cushendun, taking the minor road nearest the sea from Cushendall, over the shoulder of Cross Slieve. The light was wonderfully clear, and the wind dropped in the evening. There were splendid views over the sea.

I stayed the night at Mrs Scally's Guest house, the Villa Farm, in Cushendun, where I was very comfortable and well nourished. After my evening meal Kerry Campbell of the Northern Ireland Tourist Board called, and I had quite a long session with her, describing my journey and answering her questions.

Day 31   Friday 27 April: to Ballycastle

To-day I have walked one of the finest stretches of the Ulster Way, from Cushendun to Ballycastle, via Murlough Bay and Fairhead. My route had variety and great beauty. I started by going inland up to the old Drove Road that runs straight across the upland bog to the east of Ballypatrick Forest. This was the route taken by men driving cattle and sheep long ago, presumably on the way to Ballycastle. I had it all to myself to-day, except for the larks and an occasional curlew, and two turf-cutters away in the distance. An immense open sky arched over me, and the eye could roam in every direction. In front I had glimpses of the sea and of Rathlin Island; behind me too the sea was visible, and I had views back over the Antrim hills, where the crest of Lurigethan stood out prominently. I passed Loughaveema, the vanishing lake, which

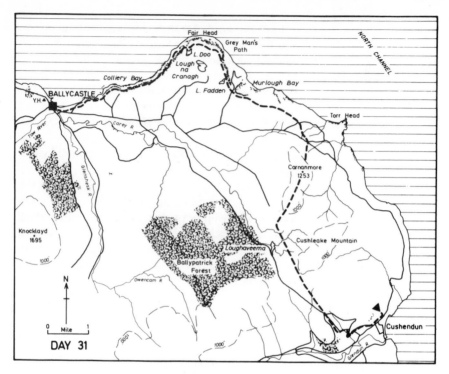

DAY 31

occasionally disappears in very dry weather. To-day
it was visibly present and seemed to have plenty of
water.

Eventually I turned off the Drove Road and
climbed up to the top of Carnanmore. Here I had
fine views over the sea and away to Scotland. I
descended northwards, moving towards the coast
then turning westwards and keeping above the
steep slopes down to the sea. Before long I could
see Murlough Bay below me. I have been many
times to this beauty spot on the north coast, which
is owned by the National Trust. Its splendour never
palls. It does not have the special geological interest
of the Giant's Causeway, but it is more beautiful and
has greater variety. The Causeway coast, although
magnificently rugged, is treeless. But here the folds
of the hills are wooded, and there are some fine
trees close to the sea. Tongues of wood push up

There is a Youth Hostel in
Ballycastle, in North
Street (closed in
February). There are also
several hotels and guest-
houses in this seaside
resort. The most famous
annual event is the 'Oul'
Lammas Fair' at the end
of August.

The beach at Cushendall, with Lurigethan behind

From Ballycastle it is possible to take a boat trip to Rathlin island. Enquire at the harbour, or at the tourist office.

The Moyle Way, a link route of the Ulster Way, runs from Ballycastle to Glenariff, over Knocklayde, up the Glenshesk valley and over Orra and Trostan. The route is waymarked with posts bearing orange arrows.

almost to the top of the scarp, but at Fair Head the naked rock plunges perpendicularly down to the sea. The Grey Man's Path offers a dramatic and fear-some-looking, but really quite simple, descent, down a steep gully to the tumbled rocks and scree below the main buttress of Fair Head.

I had no time to go down this path to-day, though it is one of my favourite cliff paths. Instead I followed the cliff tops until I was able to descend, by a small twisting goat path, to the lower route that eventually joins the road, following the edge of the sea, below Corrymeela, to Ballycastle. Just as I reached Ballycastle, about six o'clock, I was surprised and pleased to be met by Fergus Wheeler of the Moyle Council, who is Chairman of the Ulster Way Committee. He gave me a welcome lift in his car to the Antrim Arms, followed by an equally

109

Murlough Bay, with the cliffs of Fair Head, and a piece of Rathlin Island in the background

welcome pint of Guinness. We were soon joined by my wife, who had arranged to meet me here. I was now only twenty miles from Coleraine, and I had planned to spend this and the next night at home, so that I could save expenses, get some clean clothes and lighten my rucksack of things no longer needed.

Day 32   Saturday 28 April: to the Giant's Causeway

My obliging wife dropped me at the sea-front in Ballycastle at the point I had reached last night, and I followed the coast from here to the Giant's Causeway, where she collected me in the evening. It is not, in fact, possible to follow the coast the whole way. There are no rights of way over some parts of the route, and there are also natural obstacles; but I

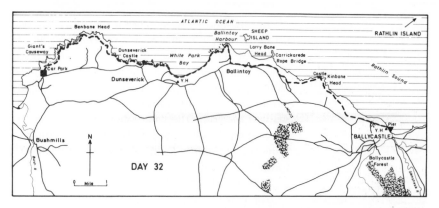

The rope bridge is used by salmon fishermen to cross a sea chasm to reach their fishing station on a small rocky island. The crossing provides an exciting venture for tourists and is very popular. The bridge is dismantled in the winter months.

kept as close as I could to the sea. I took the road through Clare Park, then cut across country, as best I could, to the car park above Kinbane Castle. This castle is built on a fine rugged head projecting into the sea, and although it was not the shortest way forward I could not resist going down the steps to it, and then climbing, by a narrow path leading westwards, up the steep grassy slopes to the top of the cliffs. From here I made my way, partly along the cliffs, partly further inland, until I reached Carrick-a-rede. I looked down on the famous rope bridge, but I went past it to join the main road above Larry Bane Head.

On the road Wilfrid Capper stopped to hail and cheer me on. He has given me unfailing support and encouragement, and now he had come to cheer me home on the last laps. Soon after he left a police car stopped and engaged me in a friendly chat. It is usually ominous when a police car stops close to you, but this time I had nothing to fear.

I was now on the hill above Ballintoy and I would like to have taken a short cut across the fields to the harbour, but I knew from previous experience that there were many high and formidable barbed-wire fences barring the way, so I walked on through Ballintoy and took the road down to the Harbour. Here I had my lunch, and once again Wilfrid caught up with me, and he took several photographs.

111

From Ballintoy I was on home ground, and I had no further need for maps, or any doubts about the best route. I have walked this part of the coast many times, but it still remains for me a splendid walk. Here it is possible to follow the coast closely the whole way, and for most of it there is a clearly marked footpath. The route offers plenty of variety: the fine sweep of White Park Bay, the tiny hamlet of Portbraddan, the ancient stump of Dunseverick Castle, and finally the rugged cliffs of Benbane Head and the Causeway itself.

As I was leaving Ballintoy I ran into a party of schoolchildren from Templemore School in Londonderry. They all asked for my autograph. This is fame at last, I thought. It was a Saturday, early in the new summer term, the season for school expeditions. Later I met a group of school girls going to the

Route along the Causeway Coast, showing White Park Bay, Portbraddon Harbour and the cliffs of Benbane Head

youth hostel at White Park Bay. They all carried huge rucksacks, and told me they were qualifying for the 'silver medal'. Later still I met another group of young ramblers. Their leader organised a cheer for me. I was somewhat embarrassed by this, but also pleased and touched.

There is a youth hostel at Whitepark Bay, above the south-western end of the beach. This is closed in November.

I had intended taking the lower path from Hamilton's Seat to the Causeway, which I prefer to the cliff-top path. This lower path must be one of the finest cliff paths in the world, and the National Trust have done a good job in building and maintaining it. Unfortunately I found a large notice at the top of the steps leading down the cliff face saying: 'It is dangerous to pass this point. Paths and steps under repair.' So reluctantly I kept to the top path and I reached the car park about six o'clock. I went into the café and the proprietress gave me a free cup of tea, which was much appreciated. Soon afterwards Hazel arrived to collect me.

Day 33   Sunday 29 April:
to Portstewart harbour

My last day—I must admit that I was relieved at the thought that my long pilgrimage was nearly over, that I would soon be able to rest my sore toe, and that I could give my mind to things other than the immediate route ahead. The day began with a minor crisis of a trivial but vexing sort. I had to return again to the Giant's Causeway, and I had planned to reach Portstewart Harbour at about four o'clock, where I knew there would be a BBC television unit waiting for me as well as friends to welcome me home. When I was all ready to set off, our car wouldn't start. After some ten minutes of unsuccessful effort I abandoned it and rang for a taxi. Then I returned to the car and tried once more; it started immediately. I was able to cancel the taxi and take the car.

113

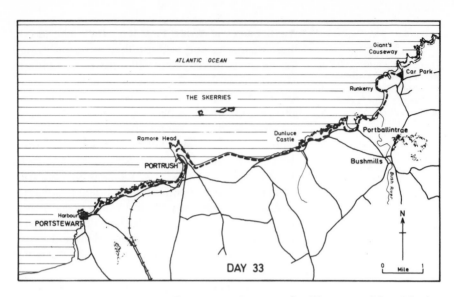

DAY 33

Once more I was on familiar ground, but I had a stiff north–westerly wind blowing in my face. I took the cliff path past Portcoon to Runkerry, then followed the old tramline to the river Bush and crossed the footbridge into Portballintrae. I followed the coastline as closely as I could, crossing the firing range (there was no red flag flying) west of Portballintrae, using the road for a short stretch before Dunluce Castle, and again before the White Rocks strand. From here I was able to walk on the beach to Portrush, where I ate my lunch in partial shelter from the wind on the steps of the Arcadia Ballroom.

I passed Portrush Harbour and walked over the sand of the West Beach, because the tide was well out. Then I took the coast path for Portstewart. Here I began to meet people I knew and I felt that I really was on the home stretch. Some of the Bannside Ramblers had come to meet me, in spite of the rain, which had now settled into a steady downpour. I had put on my full rain gear, but the rain on my spectacles gave me trouble, since the wind was blowing it in my face. I took my spectacles off for a time and put them in my pocket. As a consequence

It is possible to descend to sea-level at Portcoon, where there is a salmon fishing station. A narrow zig-zag path leads down from the cliff top.

There is a recently opened countryside centre at Portandoo on the sea-front at Portrush. This contains many exhibits relating to the north coast.

114

I almost missed Hazel on the golf course approaching Portstewart. She accompanied me towards the harbour and soon we met Wilfrid Capper and others. At the Harbour there was a group of Ramblers and well-wishers assembled in the pouring rain to greet me. Soon Patrick Burns and his television unit appeared. I gave an interview in the porch of the Carrig na Cule Hotel, conveniently situated opposite the harbour, and then there were photographs in the rain. Finally we were able to go into the hotel, and there the manager, Michael McKeever, generously presented us with hot whiskeys. So I finally drove home to Coleraine in a glow of hot whiskey and triumph. I had done the first foot-circuit of Ulster—500 miles—and was still upright and on my feet.

As I close this diary my sincere gratitude goes out to all those, both friends and strangers, who fed and sheltered and encouraged me, and helped me to keep 'right on to the end'.

Some Practical Advice for Walkers

My first point is not strictly practical but it seems to me basic to everything else. A long-distance walk is not primarily an endurance test but something to be enjoyed. It demands endurance, of course, and part of its reward is a sense of achievement, of a challenge met and conquered. But if this were all, one could achieve it by walking one thousand times round a race track. The Ulster Way has been planned to include much of the finest scenery in the north of Ireland. Give yourself time to look at it and enjoy it. My friend, Alan Coughlin from Derry, who walked the whole Way in an incredible eighteen days, would be the first to admit that much of his journey was a penance rather than a pleasure. He pushed himself too hard and had little time to linger and look about him, and he ended up with a badly swollen leg that took a month to heal. Don't make this mistake. If you cannot spend a month, or preferably more, to walk the whole Way, then choose a section of it and walk it without haste, with time to lift your eyes above and beyond the path, time to turn aside to a stone circle or an historic building, time to talk to those you meet, and to reflect on what you see and hear.

Accommodation

If you are planning to do the whole circuit, the most difficult problem is to find accommodation in the remoter areas at convenient stopping points. If you carry a tent, or decide to sleep rough, then this problem does not arise. Though there are hardly any specific camp-sites on the Way, it is easy enough to find places to pitch a tent. Most farmers, if approached, will readily grant permission for this, and there are many wilderness areas of moorland and forest, where no one will ever know you have camped, if you observe the countryside code. Of course, the weather is often unfavourable for camping. It is perhaps worth mentioning, for those prepared to sleep rough, that there are many ruined cottages and abandoned farm buildings in the Ulster countryside. It is usually possible to find some kind of shelter from the elements.

Those who, like myself, prefer a bed indoors, are advised to consult the Tourist Board booklet, *Northern Ireland: All the Places to Stay.* An up-dated version of this is issued annually. My 1982 copy is priced at sixty pence. This booklet may be obtained from the Tourist Board at River House, 48 High Street, Belfast, BT1 2DS. Sometimes travel agents have copies of the booklet, and outside Belfast the Northern Ireland Tourist Board has offices in London, the West Midlands, Scotland, North America and Europe.

In Co. Fermanagh, the Recreation Department of the District Council, which has been active in developing the Ulster Way, is very much aware of the difficulty that walkers may have in finding overnight accommodation at suitable stopping points. Anyone planning to follow the Way in Co. Fermanagh is advised to get in touch with the Recreation Officer at the Town Hall in Enniskillen (Enniskillen 3911). By prior arrangement it may be possible for the Department to provide transport to take walkers from the point where their day's journey has ended to the nearest suitable accommodation.

A fair number of youth hostels are available on the eastern and northern sections of the circuit—at Newcastle, Belfast, Ballygalley, Cushendall, Ballycastle and Whitepark Bay—but there are few in the west and south. These hostels do not provide meals, and they have little in the way of food supplies, so you need to bring your own food. Full details of the hostels will be found in the YHANI handbook, available from the Youth Hostel Association of Northern Ireland, 56 Bradbury Place, Belfast.

117

Footwear

It is difficult to decide on the best boots to wear because the route presents a wide variety of walking surfaces. There is bog and mountain, where fairly heavy waterproof boots are best, but there are also long stretches of hard surfaces on minor tarred roads, where heavy boots are less suitable. From Aughnacloy to Newry, for example, a distance of some fifty miles, walking is mainly on hard surfaces, and there are no mountains. I heard of a group who set off in heavy mountain boots to walk a portion of the Way, which they clearly knew little about, and they had to retire with blistered feet after two days' walking on hard roads. I solved the problem myself by taking two pairs of boots, a heavy pair for bog and mountain, and a light soft pair for the roads. This gave me comfort, but at the cost of extra weight in my pack. If you decide on one pair only, then choose a reasonably light, waterproof, soft boot, that will take both bog and tarred road. Whatever your preferences in footwear, give careful thought to this important aspect of the Way, and try out your boots on a variety of surfaces before you start.

Following the Waymarks

The whole idea of waymarking is to enable walkers to follow a cross-country trail without difficulty. It seems quite simple—you just follow the signs or posts provided. But my own experience has been that following waymarks is by no means as simple as it sounds. I have more than once gone astray when trying to follow a waymarked route. Several different things may create problems. The most trying of these is the removal or obliteration of signs and posts. Usually this is due to unknown vandals, but occasionally it is caused by heavy farm or forest machinery, or the rapid growth of obscuring vegetation. Sometimes you will see a post which was obviously meant to carry a sign, but with no sign there. I found this recently on the route from Newry to Rostrevor. Or you may reach a junction where there obviously should be a sign, and none is visible. All you can do is to use your map and your intuition, unless there is someone nearby to ask. I firmly believe in asking local people when I am in doubt, even if it means walking a little way to the nearest house. A local person will often be able to tell you: 'Yes, there was a sign there but it has gone. Your route is to the left and you'll find a sign at the next cross-roads.'

Even when signs have not been interfered with it is not always easy to find them. Recently I spent a good half hour looking for the first way-mark on the North Sperrin trail out of Castlerock. Sometimes one looks straight ahead in the expected direction of the trail and misses the sign to the left or the right. I can only say, 'Be patient, and keep a sharp look-out. "Seek and ye shall find."'

It should be noted that more than one style of waymark is used on the Ulster Way. The commonest is that made by the Forestry Department, a stout wooden post with an orange (sometimes faded to pale yellow) arrow indicating direction. This is used on the Lakeland Way, but in other parts of Fermanagh there is a wooden sign post with red lettering. The Department of the Environment, Roads Section, has used a metal plaque, sometimes mounted on a metal post, on the Mourne Trail— Newry to Rostrevor. At some points on the approach roads a walking man sign indicates that a section of the Way takes off from the road.

Maps

All the maps mentioned below are published by the Ordnance Survey of Northern Ireland. The prices shown are those current at the end of 1982. These maps may be obtained in bookshops, but in case of difficulty they may be ordered direct from the Ordnance Survey at 83 Ladas Drive, Belfast BT6 9FJ.

Ireland North: a holiday map, scale 1:250,000, 4 cm to 10 km, about 4 miles to the inch (price £1.50). This is too small for walking, but it is helpful in giving the general picture of Ulster. It also includes Donegal and other northern portions of the Irish Republic. The Ulster Way is marked on this map, so that it provides an over-view of the whole circuit. But the direction of the route has been changed in several places since the map was made.

Mourne Country: an outdoor pursuits map, scale 1:25,000, approx. 2½ inches to 1 mile (price £1.75). This is an excellent map and it shows clearly the section of the Ulster Way from Rostrevor to Newcastle.

These maps are now complete for Northern Ireland. Those covering Co. Donegal are not yet available, though two small sections of this county are included in maps of Coleraine (Sheet 4) and Londonderry (Sheet 7).

A first series of new large scale maps, 1:50,000, approx. 1¼ inches to 1 mile, is now in progress (price from £1.20 to £1.50). About 12 of these have already been published, and a total of 29 is planned. These will include northern parts of the Irish Republic, in particular Co. Donegal. Some of the maps show the route of the Ulster Way. They are generally very useful to walkers, but a large number will be needed to cover the whole area of the Way.

Less numerous are the older 1 inch maps (£1.25). 9 sheets cover Northern Ireland, and all 9 are required to cover the Ulster Way. These maps are naturally less up to date than the new series, but they are still very useful for the walker.

There are also ½ inch maps, covering Northern Ireland in 4 sheets (£1.25). These can be useful to show the general shape of the country.

The Sports Council of Northern Ireland

The Ulster Way was established under the guidance of the Sports Council, which has set up an Ulster Way committee to manage it. Information about the Way may be obtained from the Sports Council at the House of Sport, Upper Malone Road, Belfast, BT9 5LA. The Council has issued a leaflet of information about the Way (leaflet UW L1) and also a folder and a booklet describing the Way in general, with an outline map of the whole route. These may be obtained free from the Council, and the same goes for a series of leaflets dealing with particular sections of the Way, as follows:

For amended and updated versions of these leaflets contact the Sports Council.

The North Down Coastal Path
Belfast and Cave Hill
The Lagan Valley
The Moyle Way (loop line)
The North Antrim Coast
The Navar and Big Dog Trails (Co. Fermanagh)
The Mourne Trail (Section 1, Newry to Rostrevor)
The North Sperrin Trail (Castlerock to Dungiven)
The Gortin Trail (Gortin Village to Mellon Folk Park)
The Mourne Trail (Section 2, Rostrevor to Newcastle)

These leaflets are usually available at Countryside Centres in Northern Ireland, and at Tourist Board Offices.

Part Two

Slí Ulaidh and other Donegal Walks

Key to Maps (Part Two)

— — —	Warner's Route
═══════	Main and or Scenic Road
───────	Minor Road
—·—·—·	Border
R.Finn	River
⬭	Lake
	Sea
⣿	Land Above 300 m if not otherwise stated
▲ ▲	Forested Area
■	City
●●	Town or Village
▲ Y.H.	Youth Hostel
M	National or Ancient Monument
☀	Viewpoint

Introduction

'If you ask what is the best county in Ireland to walk in, I reply, Donegal'. So said Robert Lloyd Praeger in his classic account of his travels in Ireland, *The Way that I Went*. After exploring Donegal, off and on, for the last twenty-five years, I endorse Praeger's view whole-heartedly.

But Donegal does not lend itself to the same footpath plan that applies to Northern Ireland. It is a rugged irregular county, deeply indented by loughs and bays. Fists and fingers of land extend far out into the North Atlantic. The result of this is much striking and beautiful coastal scenery, wild and rugged; but it is not feasible to plan a circular trail that will go right round the county and take in all the scattered promontories from Slieve League to Malin Head. Instead there is one officially designated and waymarked 'Ulster Way' trail (Slí Ulaidh) running through the county from south to north, though by no means in a straight line. This trail links up with the Northern Ireland route at Pettigoe, and it runs past Lough Derg and Lough Eske, through the Blue Stack mountains to Fintown. Then, passing Lough Muck, it heads ·for the Glendowan mountains, touches the Poisoned Glen and the Glenveagh National Park, passes below Errigal round Altan Lough and finally reaches the north coast at Falcarragh. For the most part it is a true wilderness trail, penetrating remote and beautiful tracts of bog and mountain.

Apart from this trail, most of which is waymarked (though the waymarks are not always easy to follow) there are no further established trails. But there is plenty of excellent walking country. For those who like climbing, there are many hills and mountains. A guide to most of these, with routes and sketch-maps, may be found in *Irish Walk Guides 3, The North West* (Donegal/Sligo) by Simms and Foley, published in

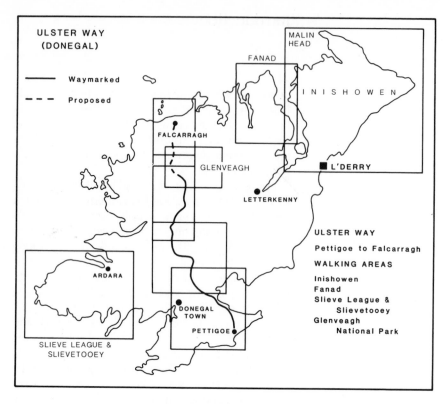

ULSTER WAY
(DONEGAL)

—— Waymarked

- - - Proposed

MALIN
HEAD

FANAD

INISHOWEN

FALCARRAGH

GLENVEAGH

L'DERRY

LETTERKENNY

ULSTER WAY

Pettigoe to Falcarragh

WALKING AREAS

Inishowen
Fanad
Slieve League &
         Slievetooey
Glenveagh
         National Park

ARDARA

DONEGAL
TOWN

PETTIGOE

SLIEVE LEAGUE &
SLIEVETOOEY

paperback by Gill & Macmillan. There are also a number of areas where walks lasting several days may be taken. Three of these are described in my journals: the Inishowen peninsula, the Fanad peninsula, and the Slieve League-Slievetooey area, which I call the Carrick Circuit. I have also included some notes on the Glenveagh National Park which offers great scope for walking.

Pettigoe to Falcarragh

Day 1   Sunday 31 March:
Pettigoe to Lough Eske

Before setting out on this five day walk, I had to work out how to reach Pettigoe at the start of the trail, and how to get home again from Falcarragh. I decided to leave my car at a friend's house in Dunfanaghy (not far from Falcarragh) and use buses to get to my starting point. I have a cousin in Laghey (not far from Pettigoe) who kindly put me up overnight and took me in his car to my starting point next morning. I was dressed in my walking gear (knee-breeches, boots, an old anorak, a rucksack and a walking-stick) when I changed buses in Derry. I was eyed very curiously by some small boys. One of them asked me, 'Are you from America?', and another, 'Are you from the hills?'!

On a dull wet Sunday morning my cousin dropped me in the middle of Pettigoe at nine. This small village, straddling the border between Co. Fermanagh and Co. Donegal, was still fast asleep. In the centre is a signpost with two wings, both inscribed 'Ulster Way', but pointing in different directions. The one pointing west indicates the route of the Northern Ireland Ulster Way, which briefly crosses the border at Pettigoe, but returns to Co. Fermanagh after two miles, crossing the Waterfoot river at Letter Bridge and winding south-west through Castle Caldwell. The other sign, pointing north along the road towards Lough Derg, is the start of the Donegal extension of the Ulster Way. This was to be my route for the next five days, leading northwards towards the coast at Falcarragh, but by no means in a straight line.

The tarred road was deserted. My only company was the sound of curlews crying. I couldn't see the birds, but their long, bubbling, melancholy cries

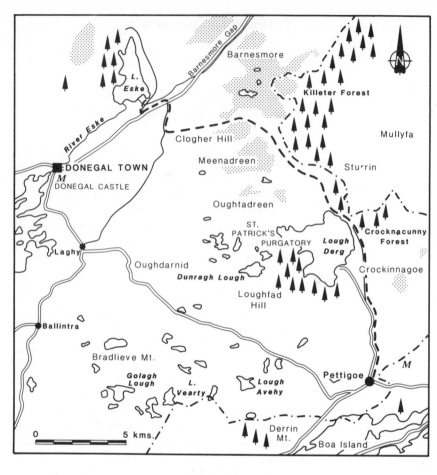

seemed the right accompaniment for the grey sky
and the wet marshy fields.

At the cross-roads, three miles from Pettigoe, I felt I
should be turning right towards the forest road,
because the route does not head straight for Lough
Derg, but goes round by its eastern shore. But the
'Walking Man' sign, used from time to time to indicate
the route, clearly pointed straight on along the road
to the Lough. I followed it and soon found myself at
the southern shore of the Lough. I could see Station
Island (St Patrick's Purgatory) across the grey, cold-

The walking man sign
was wrongly positioned.
It has now been moved
to indicate a right turn at
this point.

looking water, empty and silent. Lough Derg has been for long, and still is, a very important shrine for devout Catholic pilgrims, but the pilgrim season does not begin until May.

Several Irish writers have described Lough Derg and the penitential practices of the pilgrims visiting Station Island. In 1850 the Ballyshannon poet, William Allingham, paid a visit as a 'non-pilgrim eye-witness'. He told how the pilgrims went into 'Prison' on the second night, fasting, praying and keeping awake all night. Next morning they were revived with bread and wine, but the 'wine' was merely the boggy-flavoured water of the lake, drunk hot. At the end of his visit Allingham remarked: 'Twas but a matter of twenty miles or less, yet we seemed to have driven home out of the Middle Ages'.

Nearly a hundred years later Patrick Kavanagh paid a visit to the island, and he later wrote a long poem about it entitled *Lough Derg*. Sean O'Faolain used the place as the basis of one of his best-known short stories, 'Lovers of the Lake', in which two sophisticated lovers are profoundly affected by a visit to the island.

I realised that I had gone off the trail, so, still meditating on Lough Derg, I plunged down into the bog and heather, and walked towards the forest on the east side of the Lough. Before long I struck the road that I should have taken, and I followed it into the forest. But my problems of route-finding were not over. The route was waymarked with stout wooden posts, about six inches in diameter, with the top half painted white. On some posts the paint had worn off; other posts had almost fallen over, and I saw one that had been used to mend a fence. But I managed to find my way through the forest and out on to a newly-made rough road running towards Kelly's Bridge. This road eventually joined the road running from the Donegal town direction to Kelly's Bridge. It divides two areas of forestry plantation. The Ulster Way goes west along this road for a few yards, then follows a boggy fire-break northwards towards Lough Eske and the Blue Stack mountains. At the end of the fire-break there is a river. On a previous occasion I had been able to jump over it, but now the rain had swollen it, and jumping was not possible. Reluctantly I took off my boots and waded through. The water was decidedly cold, but this was a small hardship compared with the trouble of drying feet and putting on socks and boots again, which took some time.

Soon another river crossed my path, but this one I was able to jump, after first throwing over my rucksack. Then it was easier going over open bog until I reached the end of the track running below the northern side of Clogher Hill. Here there was a car parked and two farmers were out looking for sheep. They were the first people I had encountered since a forestry van passed me near Lough Derg. I had seen no signs of human habitation since then, and hardly any sheep. But now a few small farms began to appear below me.

This part of the route offered me some splendid views. To the north the Blue Stack mountains were now fully visible, with wreaths of mist on the summits, and away to the west I could see Donegal Bay and the Atlantic beyond it. Before long I reached a tarred road, and I followed this down till it joined the main Donegal-Ballybofey Road below Barnesmore Gap. My destination was Mrs McGinty's Guest House at Ardeevin, on the road running round the east side of Lough Eske. Ardeevin can be reached by following down the main road for about a mile, then turning right and right again, but I knew it was possible to take a short cut by crossing the Barnes river and joining the road that runs above it on the other side of the valley. When I had looked at the river on a previous occasion it had seemed easy enough to cross, but now I knew it would be in flood. In spite of this I decided to take the short cut and avoid the main road. When I came to the river it was clear that I must wade through it, but I was reluctant to spend time getting my boots off and on again, so, since I was near the end of my day's tramp, and my feet were already thoroughly wet, I decided to walk through the river with my boots on. It was only when I was squelching along the bank on the other side that I remembered the difference between walking with wet feet and walking with one's boots full of water. But I plodded on to Ardeevin, where I was glad to take off my boots outside Mrs McGinty's front door and pour the water out of them.

Later that evening, when I was telling Mrs McGinty about my day's walk, she said to me; 'You must be a glutton for punishment'. I was to chew over this remark a good deal in the following days

---

Day 2   Monday 1 April: to Commeen

The sky was overcast and there was soft rain falling as I set out at nine this morning, making for Edergole and the Blue Stacks. At Edergole I took refuge for a few minutes in a shed while I changed a jersey. Outside I suddenly heard the song of a robin, and I recalled a four-line poem by John Pick.

> Rough tongues of winter
> Then this robin's song
> Like a quick drink of silence
> Under the bawling wind.

Likening a song to 'a quick drink of silence' is strange and baffling, but it is memorable.

I passed another shed where a man was milking a cow by hand. This old method of milking still persists, but it is no longer common. Even on remote hill farms the milking machine is replacing human hands.

The path I was about to ascend, which follows the Corrober river up into the mountains, is known as 'the monks path'. Partly to ask about this, and partly because the mist was still down on the hills, I called at the last small farm on the hillside. There was a car

131

outside the door, and a TV aerial on the roof. The hill farms are no longer as remote from the rest of the world as they once were. Nobody in the house knew much about the monks who used the path through the Blue Stacks, but the woman of the house very kindly made me tea, and wished me luck on my journey.

I went on upstream, following the waymarks, easy to find on this part of the route. Before long I came to the point where the river running down from Lough Belshade joins the Corrober river. On previous occasions I had crossed it without difficulty, but this time it was in full spate, so I had to walk up the bank, searching for a possible crossing. Only when I reached the edge of Lough Belshade did I find one. Here there was a tiny island in midstream, big enough to take two feet, and there was a half-submerged rock in front of it. I threw over my stick and rucksack, and then made the crossing by a kind of hop, step and jump, without getting my feet in the water. To celebrate my successful crossing I treated myself to a tot of whisky from my small emergency flask, and decided to have lunch on a small sandy beach at the edge of the Lough.

Although I was off the direct route, I was glad that I had come up to Lough Belshade. It is a most beautiful Lough, surrounded on three sides by steep mountains. The rain had stopped, and though there was still mist on the hills, it was lifting. Far off on the water I saw two mysterious white birds. When the visibility improved I realised that they were swans. I was surprised, because I had not expected to find swans so high up in the mountains.

As I turned down towards the Corrober river the rain came on again, and the mist made it difficult to see the waymarking posts at the top of the pass. But I managed to keep to the route, and I followed the posts down the hillside to the Owendoo river.

This river valley was really sodden, and walking through it was like walking on a vast sponge. I was glad to reach a hard surface when I joined the road at

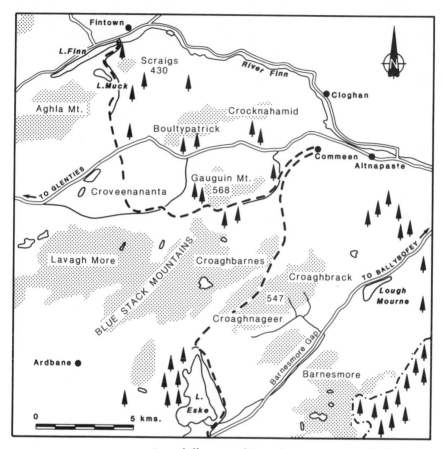

Letterkillew. At this point I turned aside from the
Ulster Way towards my night's lodging. I had found
accommodation in the small village of Commeen.
This is an Irish-speaking village in a small pocket of
the Gaeltacht. When I called here to enquire about
accommodation I was addressed in Irish, which, alas,
I don't know. I can't recall ever being addressed in
Irish before, although I have lived now for 24 years in
Ireland, and before coming to live here I had visited
it many times. The Doherty's, with whom I stayed the
night, spoke Irish as their first language, and they
sometimes had students of Irish staying with them,
but of course they were fluent in English too. Mrs

133

Doherty told me of an amusing incident when they were on a visit to Spain. They saw a man reading the *Daily Mail,* and said, in Irish, that he must be a Sassenach. The man turned round and replied: 'Ah'm no Sassenach, Ah'm a Scotsman'.

Mrs Doherty also told me that she had three times been as a pilgrim to Lough Derg. She said that the discipline of penance — going without shoes, fasting and keeping awake all night — was hard, but it made you feel good afterwards. This comment, too, gave me food for thought next day.

Day 3   Tuesday 2 April:
to Fintown

I walked up the road I had come down the evening before, to Letterkillew, to rejoin the route of the Ulster Way. The waymarking posts follow up the south side of the Owengarve river, but I was advised to take the forest road, on the north side of the river, instead. This road runs round the lower slopes of Gaugin mountain, through plantations of conifers. Trees were being felled and stacked in the forest. I passed a timber-hauling machine standing idle. The operators were sitting in a car nearby, having a tea-break. Later on I passed three empty cars near a wooden hut. The door of the hut was shut, but I heard voices and smelt tobacco. Another tea-break? As I climbed out of the mature plantation I saw what work they were engaged in. At the side of the road was a spade and a bag of pine saplings. They were planting trees on a cold wet hillside. I could well understand their taking refuge for a time in a snug wooden hut.

I was still on the forest road, which began to turn north round the shoulder of Gaugin mountain, and I knew that I must rejoin the waymarked route, which ran outside the forest boundary. I could see a white post on the hillside, so I left the road and walked through a newly-planted piece of the forest — heavy going for a time over hummocks and ditches — until I was out of the forest and heading for the bridge across the Reelan river. I was now going through the area known locally as the 'Croaghs', and for a time I was on the road running towards Glenties.

It was raining slightly and there was a cold wind blowing, so I sought shelter in a roofless cottage. I sat in the old open fireplace, because the chimney offered some partial shelter, and enjoyed my bread and cheese and apple, and a flask of hot coffee. After lunch I followed the route, which soon left the road, up a bleak and boggy hillside towards the slopes of Croveenanta. At one point I was followed by a flock of hungry sheep, who evidently thought I was bringing food for them.

On a previous exploratory walk I had lost the waymarks on this section. The nature of the ground, which fell away from the highest point, with hillocks and small ravines, made them difficult to follow. This time I was very careful, and I managed to find the posts all the way to the road below — the road from Ballybofey to Glenties, passing via Commeen. The rest of my way to Fintown was easy to follow. First I was on a track running through bogland, where I flushed an unexpected woodcock; and then I was on a tarred road, running past Lough Muck, over the lower slopes of Scraigs mountain and round Lough Finn to the long straggling village of Fintown.

As I walked this easy route I meditated on pilgrimages and other ways of mortifying the flesh. Was I really a glutton for punishment, as Mrs McGinty had said? Is there a streak of masochism in undertaking long walks in uncertain weather? There is certainly more than a streak of masochism in some of the practices encouraged by Irish Catholicism, not only the hard-ships of Lough Derg, but practices like self-flagellation and the wearing of chains. There seems to be a morbid side to this. In his autobiography, the Irish poet, Austin Clarke, writes about one of his teachers, Father Boyle, who was forbidden long fasts by the conditions of community life, so he devised private methods of mortifying the flesh. 'He tried to cut the

135

Holy Name of Jesus on his chest with a razor blade but suffered too much loss of blood, and the application of a heated iron caused ugly dangerous sores. His last attempt was almost fatal. He was giving a Retreat in a Convent near Greystones and one evening, passing a lonely wood, he saw a bed of nettles. Hastily stripping, he jumped into the bed, rolled among the nettles and was severely poisoned'.

I find this story horrifying. My reaction is similar to what I have read about the self-inflicted hardships of Matt Talbot, declared Venerable by the Church in 1976. After giving up drinking, he led an austere life, sleeping on a wooden plank, with a wooden block for a pillow. When he died it was discovered that he wore a chain round his waist, and others on his arm and leg.

At the same time I think some mortification of the flesh may be a healthy and not a morbid thing, healthy both physically and spiritually. The Christian pilgrims of the past who walked long distances and endured hardships to visit a holy place must have been strengthened by a new sense of dedication and blessing. Even a secular pilgrimage, like my own, brings its rewards in a sense of achievement, and an awareness of penetrating deeply into the wild places of the earth.

Day 4   Wednesday 3 April:
to Dunlewy

I left Fintown before nine because I knew I had a long haul through lonely upland bog in an area where I had previously had difficulty in finding the waymarks. I was heading for the Glendowan mountains, and I started off along a farm track to the north-east of Fintown that ran in the direction of Lough Muck. (Yet another Lough Muck! The name is derived from *muc,* the Irish for pig, and is common in Ireland). The track passed a number of small hill farms, some of them abandoned and ruined, but others still inhabited. Near the end of the track I passed a farmer wheeling a turf-barrow. We both stopped for a brief chat. He told me that he had no electricity because many years ago, when more of these cottages were inhabited, the other householders had declined an offer from the E.S.B. to supply electricity, thinking it too expensive, and so a supply line was never established. I thought what a lonely life this man must lead. He had no car, no television, and most of the cottages near him were abandoned and empty. The back hills of Donegal must surely contain some of the loneliest dwellings in Ireland, and indeed in the world.

The track ended at a deserted cottage, which was still roofed with corrugated iron, though the ceiling plaster had fallen inside. There were a few chairs in the living room, a cloth still on the table, and a mug. These homely objects seemed to emphasise the desolation of an abandoned home. At this point the waymarks began, and the route turned north at a right angle heading into the open bog. I managed to find the posts this time, with some difficulty, until I got beyond Lough Muck, then I missed them and climbed up too far to the east. I sensed that I was on the wrong track and turned more to the west. Then I spotted a single post on the hillside above me and I got back on to the line, after quite a wide detour. I followed the posts down to the road running from Churchill to Doocharry, below Meenbog hill. At this point the waymarks ended, but the route goes on to the north, through the Ballaghgeeha Gap and on towards Errigal. I was going off the route to my night's lodging in Dunlewy, so I intended to follow down the Poisoned Glen until I reached the road.

This sinister-sounding name is derived from the poisonous Irish Spurge *(genus Euphorbia)*. This was reputed to have grown along the banks of the Cronaniv Burn, which drains this marshy glen.

It was now growing late, so I thought I would try a short cut. Instead of going round through the Ballyaghaeeha Gap, I would try to find a gulley that leads directly down through the steep buttresses that close in the head of the Glen. I had twice been up this gulley, which is clearly visible from below, but I had never been down it. I completely failed to find

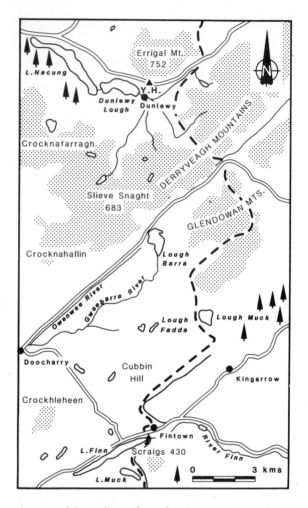

the top of the gulley. After a fruitless search I realised I was wasting time, so I turned back towards the Ballaghgeeha Gap. Then I saw, not far from the deer fence that encloses the Glenveagh National Park, what seemed a possible way down. I couldn't quite be sure there would be no sudden drop at the bottom end, but I took a chance and fortunately I was able to get right down without difficulty. Then it was a wet, sloppy slog down the Poisoned Glen, until I hit the road near the ruined church in Dunlewy. It was now eight o'clock and already dark.

As I stepped on to the road I saw a car coming towards me. It was my host, Mr Doherty, and his son, who had come out to look for me. I had let them know beforehand the route I was taking and I had expected to reach Dunlewy before dark. I was not sorry to get a lift along the last piece of road, towards shelter, warmth and food. I remembered again those lines of Edward Thomas in his poem 'The Owl', a poem that must surely appeal to all walkers.

> Downhill I came, hungry, and yet not starved;
> Cold, yet had heat within me that was proof
> Against the North wind; tired, yet so that rest
> Had seemed the sweetest thing under a roof.

Day 5   Thursday 4 April: to Falcarragh

This was an easy day after yesterday's long slog through wilderness country. I had much less distance to cover, and although there were no signs or waymarks on this section of the route, there were definite features to guide me, such as Errigal mountain and Altan Lough. I set off along the tarred road to Glenveagh to re-join the route, which keeps above the Poisoned Glen to the east, but eventually reaches the road. This road affords fine mountain views on both sides. To the north is Errigal and the Aghlas, and to the south lies the Derryveagh range. About two miles from Dunlewy, I turned off the road at the gate marked 'Altan Farm'. Here there is a winding track leading to the shore of Altan Lough. There is no longer a farm here, but a square stone keep, a kind of Folly, stands where the river flows into the Lough. The walk along this track is a pleasant one, with vistas of mountains opening out as one travels on.

The river running into the Lough was in spate, but I had no difficulty this time. A splendid row of large

139

Errigal Mountain, Co. Donegal

square stones provided an easy crossing. I sat for a time at the base of the keep, eating an orange and looking at the Lough. I was amused at the behaviour of some sheep grazing near the edge of the Lough. There was a tiny green island, which clearly offered good grazing, separated from the Lough shore by a few feet of water. The sheep were looking at it, but I thought they would not venture to cross the water, because sheep are such timid creatures. But suddenly one of them took a jump and splashed through the water to the little island of green grass. After some hesitation, the others followed, one by one, and I left them enjoying their new pasture.

My route was now round the east side of Altan Lough, below the green slopes of Aghla More. I looked across the Lough to Errigal, with steep slopes of scree falling from its summit. Soon I had glimpses of the sea beyond Falcarragh. At Proclis, a small cluster of farms, I crossed the Tullaghobegly river, that runs out of the north end of Altan Lough, by some convenient stepping-stones, and soon I was on a lane leading to Falcarragh. Falcarragh was the end of my route, and I had planned to take a bus from

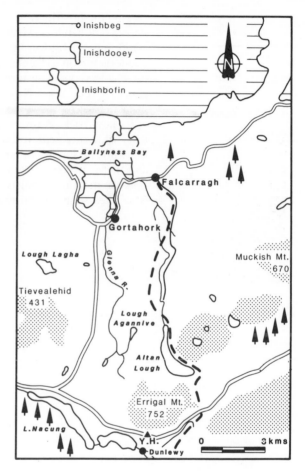

there to Dunfanaghy to reach my car. But I knew there was a bus strike. If I was stranded I thought I could probably find a taxi, but I decided I would first try to hitch-hike along the coast road.

At the crossroads in Falcarragh I fortified myself with a pint of Guinness, and then I took up a position on the road to Dunfanaghy and lifted my thumb. The first car that saw me slowed, then stopped, some way ahead of me. I watched it, but after a few seconds it went on again. Did the driver not like the look of me, or did he have an argument with his wife about picking me up? The next car stopped and gave me a lift, but only a mile down the road. I took up a strategic position near a bridge, and soon another car stopped and took me on to Dunfanaghy. Here I collected my car, changed out of my heavy boots, and drove home, glad to have completed the first lap of the Ulster Way in Donegal.

Looking back on my walk I felt this route to be a true wilderness trail, through beautiful and varied, but wild and lonely country. There are several roads and tracks, but no well-trodden paths, such as one finds on the long-distance paths in England. Anyone who likes solitude and wild places will enjoy this trail.

The Fanad Peninsula

Day 1 Saturday 24 May:
Milford to Portsalon

I stayed overnight in Milford and left my car there. This morning I left my B & B base at 8.10 a.m. and walked south along the road to Ramelton and Letter-kenny, for a short distance. Almost immediately I found myself passing the Catholic church, designed in 1961 by Corr & McCormick. I wondered if it would be open at this early hour, and I decided to pay a quick visit. It was open, but quite empty. I liked the simple, spare, diagonal rows of seats and the uncluttered feel of the place. The stained glass and the reredos tapestry by Colin Middleton harmonised with this feeling, and I particularly liked the small, simple ceramic stations of the cross by Imogen Stuart.

I soon turned off the main road to the left, past the local cattle-mart. Behind this complex of sheds there still stands the ruined shell of the old Workhouse. I was struck by the sharp contrast between the old and the new. Behind rose the elegant frame of the Georgian building, with a graceful arched doorway and fine corbelled chimney stacks, and right in front of it was a great gaunt corrugated-iron shed, purely functional and blankly ugly.

I followed the lane uphill, moving eastwards across the peninsula towards Lough Swilly. There was no traffic at all, and I was able to study the hedgerows. Although we had had a late cold spring, the hedges were greening. The blackthorn was just beginning to show its white blossom, and the whin bushes (gorse) were a bright blaze of yellow. But the buds on the ash-trees were still furled, and I recalled a phrase from Synge's play, *The Playboy of the Western World*. Christy, the hero, speaks of his old father going out at night after a drinking bout, 'as

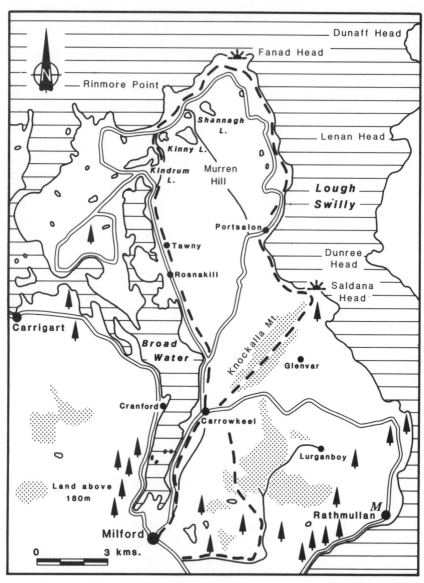

naked as an ash-tree in the moon (month) of May'.
This line, which has the rhythm of poetry, though it
occurs in prose dialogue, always comes to my mind
when I look at an ash-tree in May. Although some

ash-trees in sheltered places do show their leaves in May, the majority are still naked enough.

There were some wild violets showing their blooms in the hedgerows, and soon I was cheered by the sight of a small white butterfly. A little later I came across a more unusual sight, a completely black rabbit.

After following this pleasant lane for about a mile and a half I came to a crossroads and here I turned left. Just past the turn I noticed a ruined cottage, a sight all too common in Donegal. This one still had a good roof, though all the glass had been knocked out of the windows. One room was being used to store straw and it struck me that it would be a warm dry place to sleep, if one was benighted in this place. After passing the cottage my road climbed up a hill-side and then brought me down to Glentidally. On the way down I could see the roofs of Glenalla House, surrounded by woods. This is one of the Big Houses, homes of the Anglo-Irish gentry, of which there are several in the Fanad Peninsula.

A few yards past the St Columbkille's Church of Ireland church I turned right towards the hills, and soon afterwards went left to follow the so-called 'Green Road' through the hills past Crockanafrin mountain. Since this part of the country is unfamiliar to me I decided to ask about the route at a house, where I saw a girl getting into a car. When I asked about Crockanafrin she told me that she had never heard of it. It seemed strange to me that someone should live out in the country and not know the name of the mountain above her house. I had better luck at the next house I tried, where a man confirmed my identification of Crockanafrin and advised me to take the track to the left of it. I did this and soon came in sight of Carrowkeel, often called Kerrykeel, and the Knockalla range of mountains, which I was heading for. After a while I left the turf-track I was following and cut across country to ascend the Knockalla range at a point about a mile from Carrow-keel.

Once up on the ridge I had fine views in all

directions. Although the sky was sombre and overcast, the visability was quite good. I could see Lough Swilly in front of me and Mulroy Bay behind me. Two beautiful small loughs nestle in the Knockalla hills, roughly in the middle of the range, between the two main summits (un-named) but they are not visible until one comes close above them. After the loughs I kept to the north-west side of the ridge, heading for Ballymastocker Bay. As I descended a steady rain began to fall, not heavy but very persistent. Below Saldahna Head I looked around for some possibility of shelter. The only thing that offered itself was the public lavatory on the main road, not far from the beach. The iron gate of the Gents looked to me as if it was open, but a few minutes before I reached the building a man drove up in a car, got out and locked it. I was not very disappointed because a lavatory hardly offers desirable shelter. I found some temporary relief from the rain on the leeward side of the building, and here I put on my oilskin trousers in preparation for the open beach.

Ballymastocker beach offers a fine open stretch of firm sand, running for about two miles towards Portsalon. It is delightful to walk on, and it provides a complete change from the ridge of hills. Even in the rain I enjoyed it, and I was fortunate enough to see several gannets fishing not far from the shore. A diving gannet is a splendid sight that never fails to thrill me. From high above the water, where it is flying and watching for its prey below, it suddenly turns and plummets into the sea, sending up a white spume of spray. After a few seconds it emerges again and continues flying, having presumably caught and swallowed a small fish or eel. I believe that small eels are the gannet's favourite food.

There are two obstacles to the walker's progress along this fine open strand. Two rivers run into the sea, one at each end of the bay. The first one I was able to walk through at its shallowest point, where it entered the sea. The other, below the Golf Course at Portsalon, was deeper. I followed its winding course inland for about half a mile until I found a small bridge erected for the convenience of golfers. I crossed it and continued to walk away from the beach until I reached Mrs Kathleen Duffy's Guest House, which is on the main coastal road leading to Portsalon. This was my base for the night, and I was glad to find refuge from the rain that was still falling.

Day 2   Sunday 25 May: to Ballyhernan

The rain had ceased, and although there was a fresh cool breeze, there were bright gleams of sunshine. I took the road through Portsalon and continued northwards, following the coast towards Fanad Head. As I climbed up the hill from Portsalon I had splendid views over the blue waters of Lough Swilly to Dunree Head and the Urris hills beyond it. Nearer at hand there were masses of yellow whins on the rough hillside. The road descended through trees and tongues of wood. Everywhere there was luxuriant growth. The young ash-trees were in leaf, and I noticed wild strawberries which had seeded themselves on top of a low wall. Near the entrance to Carrablagh House I glimpsed a magnolia tree in full flower, and beside it was a fine tree with red leaves. Was it a copper beech? I couldn't see it very clearly from the road, so I started to walk along the drive towards the house, but I soon came to a notice saying PRIVATE — BEWARE OF DOG. I decided that curiosity might lead me into trouble, and that I was straying from my proper route, so I returned to the road and went on my way.

Some weeks later, when I was passing Carrablagh House, I met a young woman coming out of the drive. She told me that the tree with red leaves was a Japanese plane.

Soon I arrived at a point above the Seven Arches. There is no sign or marker to indicate this curious rock-formation on the shoreline, about four hundred yards below the road, but I had previously enquired my way from a local man, and I knew where to turn off. There is a group of buildings on the right, including a large corrugated iron shed, which bears a name-plate marked KEENAN BROS. LTD., BAGANALS-

147

TOWN. About two fields below this is the rugged shoreline. There is a steep drop down to the rocky beach, alongside a small stream, which sprays down over the cliff as a waterfall. Here a profusion of wild flowers were growing, including late primroses still in full bloom, and wild violets. As a tourist attraction, or a natural curiosity, I found the Seven Arches something of a let-down. I could see only two or three arches of rock, and since I am mostly ignorant of geology, I didn't find them very exciting. Apparently it is only at low tide that all seven arches are visible.

It is not possible to follow the shoreline direct from the Seven Arches, so I climbed up the fields again to enquire my way to the beach at Drumnacraig Strand. I knocked at the door of a small farmhouse, and a polite and friendly old man walked with me to a gate where he could point out the route. I went on over pleasant green sward down onto a sandy beach. So far I had met no other walkers, but here on the beach I overtook a young couple from Derry, with two small children. They were spending the weekend in a holiday house near the beach.

At this point I remembered Mrs Edna Wharton, whose house was close at hand. She was formerly secretary of the Fanad Development Association, and she had helped me with local information. I knocked at her door and was given a friendly welcome together with a cup of coffee and more useful information. The Whartons originally come from Yorkshire, but have long been settled in Fanad.

Soon I was back on the shore, heading for the Great Arch. This is a spectacular rock formation: a huge arch standing out from the shore, though joined to it by a rugged, rocky platform, over which the tides toss and sweep. The tide was now low, so I was able to scramble right to the base of the arch. I remembered Mrs Wharton telling me that she had once climbed to the top of this rock in her youth, but I could see no way up that could be tackled without a rope, so I scrambled back to the shore and headed north for the lighthouse.

At this point the shoreline was too steep and

rugged to be followed, so I went inland for a time, following an old boreen past a group of deserted farm buildings and then striking up a heathery slope to the skyline above Pollet Head. I climbed, with great care, a really formidable barbed-wire fence, and then I found a turf-track, which I was able to follow all the way to Fanad Head. After I had gained a little more height a splendid panoramic view opened before me, revealing the lighthouse and the whole northern coastline of Fanad, with the Atlantic stretching away into the distance. To the east was the mouth of Lough Swilly, Dunaff Head, and away beyond it Malin Head, the northernmost tip of Ireland. To the west lay Melmore Head and Horn Head, and further inland the pig's back of Muckish, and the sharp triangular peak of Errigal. The turf-track took a winding course through upland bog towards Fanad Head. It was a fine scenic route, marred only by the occasional unsightly dump of household rubbish. Clearly this unfrequented track, away from human

Fanad Head lighthouse, overlooking the Atlantic, offers excellent views of the northern coastline

habitation, had proved a tempting place to dump a load of unwanted junk, from battered armchairs to broken-down refrigerators.

Eventually the track led me down to the cluster of houses at Fanad Head, about half a mile above the lighthouse. It was now lunchtime, so I called in at the Lighthouse Tavern, where I was able to get a shepherd's pie with a glass of Guinness. The small bar was not crowded — just one elderly local man having a long Sunday drink, and a young couple from England, who were making a quick tour of Ireland.

After lunch I went down to have a look at the light-house. Next to it was the gaunt, windowless, concrete shell of an old coastguard station, burnt out in the 'troubles' of 1920. At the entrance to the light-house was a notice saying that only those with a permit from the Irish Lights authority could go in. So I went down to the edge of the cliffs opposite the lighthouse and settled down to watch the sea-birds. Over a deep inlet of the sea I looked across to some old steps, leading down to the water below. Half way down these steps, on the side of the cliff, there were two nesting gulls. I thought I could reach at least one of these by going down the steps. So I called in at the lighthouse (the gate was shut but not locked) and asked the caretaker if I might go down the steps to see the nests. He gave me permission and told me that the nesting birds were common gulls, now becoming increasingly less common.

I was able to reach the first nest without much difficulty. The sitting gull flew off, revealing two beautiful mottled eggs, resting on a wisp of grass on a small rocky ledge. After a quick admiring look, I moved away, to allow the agitated mother bird, wheeling and crying above me, to return to her nest and continue in peace her task of hatching the eggs.

I now left the road and continued my route south-westwards by walking over the grassy sand-dunes close to the sea. The shore itself was mostly rocky and stony, so I kept just above it. I encountered a good many fences, but none of them were high or difficult. There were many sea-birds, also lapwings, and I startled three Irish hares. The smell of the sea was strong, and frequently I saw pieces of sea-litter blown far in by the strong winds. At one point I encountered a large red plastic buoy, still apparently undamaged, blown half-a-mile inland from the sea.

In the Rinmore area I found myself crossing a vast rabbit-warren. The rabbits did not seem very shy, or alarmed at my approach. Some of them sat, or stood on their hindlegs, watching my approach, and only bolted down their burrows when I got close. Rabbits were once sold freely in the butchers' shops in Ireland, but since the spread of myxomatosis people are reluctant to eat them. Perhaps this is why they are multiplying so freely in places such as this.

I reached my shelter for the night at Claggan House, Ballyhernan, just as the rain was beginning to fall. So far I had enjoyed a fine day, with a good deal of sunshine and excellent visibility. The rain now falling outside gave added zest to my indoor pleasures: a hot bath, clean clothes and the prospect of food.

Day 3 Monday 26 May: to Milford

The rain had ceased in the night, and I set out soon after nine on a clear, fresh morning. I was now walking south back to my starting point in Milford. But instead of following the main road past Fanavolty church to Kindrum, I turned right up a lane alongside Claggan House, intending to make a diversion round Lough Kindrum. The lane soon petered out, so I took a line across country over a hill where there were vivid yellow whin bushes and also bluebells and primroses. I steered by the lough below me until I reached the road running west towards Kindrum. I was still following round the edge of the irregular lough, and at one point I saw what seemed to be gulls nesting on old tree-stumps standing in the water. I was surprised because I thought that gulls always nested on cliffs above the sea. I met a man working on the road, so I asked him about it, and he confirmed that they were indeed nesting gulls.

At the point where I joined the main road again, having made a circuit round Lough Kindrum, I saw a stone memorial. I went to look at it and found that the inscription was in Irish on one side and in English on the other. The English version read as follows:

ERECTED TO THE MEMORY
OF THE THREE FANAD PATRIOTS
NEIL SHIELS, DOUGHMORE
MICHAEL HERAGHTY, TULLYCONNELL
MICHAEL McELWEE, BALLYWHORISKEY
WHO BY THEIR HEROISM
IN CRATLAGH-WOOD
ON THE MORNING OF APRIL 2nd 1878
ENDED THE TYRANNY OF LANDLORDISM

I followed the road south through Kindrum, and before long I found myself looking down on what seemed to be a fish farm in the waters of Mulroy Bay. This section of the very irregular bay is known as North Water, and I was in fact looking down on the Fanad Fisheries. I was curious to know what kind of fish were being farmed so I walked down to a place where I could see a group of men working. They were in the hatcheries, decanting the swarming fry into large containers to ship them out to the main farm in the bay. The place was, in fact, a large salmon farm. Since I knew I would be returning home in the evening it occurred to me that I might perhaps buy a small salmon and take it with me in my rucksack. I was referred to the office, and there I was told to go to a large shed on the waterside, where the salmon were prepared for the market. I walked down to the shed where great heaps of gleaming salmon were being handled, but I soon found that the smallest fish available weighed over 7 kilos, and I knew I would regret the extra weight in my rucksack at the end of the day. So I decided to call again at the farm when I had my car.

On 2 April 1878 the third Earl of Leitrim was murdered, together with his clerk and his driver, as they passed through Cratlagh Wood, on the west shore of Mulroy Bay. The Earl was a man of violent temper. He tried to improve his large estates in Donegal, but he had evicted many of his tenants and was threatening others. He declined to recognise the traditional Ulster Tenant-Right custom, and feeling against him was especially strong in Fanad. Following the murders three men were arrested, including Heraghty, who died of fever in jail before trial. The other two were released because there was insufficient evidence against them. Shiels and McElwee were never arrested, although a £500 reward was offered for information. This memorial was erected in 1960.

After this interlude I continued to follow the road south. Before long I came to a substantial but ruined building. It bore the date 1909, and looked like a church or chapel. After passing it I decided to leave the road, which ran alongside the bay, and climb up the hillside on my left to get a better view of the countryside ahead. I did get a better view, but I soon came down again from the hills because the freshening wind had become very cold. So I followed the coast road to Tamnay, and then continued along the road to Rossnakill. It was still cold, so I decided to eat my lunch indoors. I went into 'Jimmy's Bar', ordered a drink and asked if I might eat my lunch there. Jimmy readily agreed, and I sat at one end of the room eating my sandwiches, while a group of local men sat around the turf fire at the other end, drinking and discussing world politics. Among them was the local postman. Presumably he had finished his day's round, and he was now getting drunk. This lent colour, but also some confusion, to the discussion. Amongst the group was a young German who had apparently settled in Fanad. I listened to the conversation, which was carried on aloud, with considerable interest. It was more entertaining, if less informative, than a news bulletin, and eventually I found myself being drawn into it. But I was conscious of the long road ahead and I soon took my leave.

I continued south, following the road to Carrowkeel. After crossing Keadue bridge the road runs along the part of Mulroy Bay known as Broad Water. There are pleasant open views across the water, but a tarred road is seldom the happiest route for a walker.

Carrowkeel is a pleasant little village, offering accommodation and refreshment to travellers. I had a pot of tea at 'The Village Restaurant' and then followed the road again towards Milford. I had views of the bay and its many islands as I walked along close to the water. At Milford Bakery I saw a large group of swans. Apparently they have been here for many years, thriving on Milford bread. After passing the large Bakery at the water's edge, I was soon back in Milford, where I collected my car and drove home.

153

Although my third day had been mostly spent walking on tarred roads. I left Fanad with the strong conviction that this small peninsula has a great deal to offer to those who explore it on foot.

The Inishowen Peninsula

Day 1 Sunday 6 June: Derry to Buncrana

I started my walk today at the Guildhall in the centre of Londonderry, underneath the famous city walls that withstood the long siege of 1689. This seemed the right place to start since Londonderry is the natural gateway to Inishowen. I planned to walk

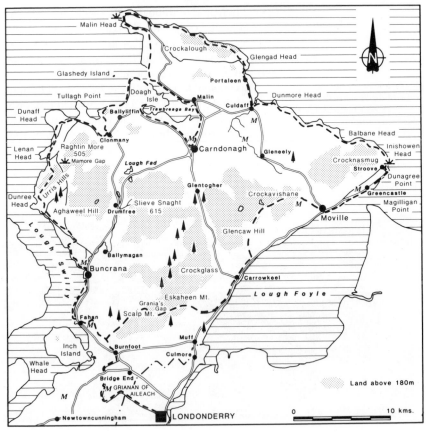

clockwise round the peninsula, so I was now aiming for Buncrana. The direct route from Derry to Buncrana is by a busy and not very interesting main road, so I chose a more devious but much more interesting route.

I turned off the main artery of the Strand Road into Clarendon Street, a wide and noble street, with some fine Georgian facades. At the top of this street I turned right into Northland Road, and passing at the back of Magee College (now part of the University of Ulster) I came to Glen Road, which leads up towards the hills above Derry. Finally I turned right into Groarty Road, which runs straight across the border below the Grianan of Aileach. There is no checkpoint here and nothing to stop a walker crossing into the Republic of Ireland, though the road is blocked against cars. After two miles along pleasant deserted lanes I reached the ancient ring-fort on a hilltop known as the Grianan of Aileach.

This ancient fort is a large dry-stone cashel, circular in shape and about $17\frac{1}{2}$ feet high, with its outer walls sloping slightly inwards. The walls had worn down over the years, but they were built up and restored in

The ancient ring-fort, Grainan of Aileach, with fine panoramic views over the surrounding countryside

the 1870s by a local enthusiastic scholar and anti-quarian, Dr Walter Bernard. The fort dates back into the mists of legend, and it was the chief stronghold of the local king for many centuries, until it was finally sacked and destroyed by the King of Munster in AD 1101. It is still an impressive memorial to the past, and it commands a fine panoramic view of the surrounding country on every side.

The inside of the fort, where the grassy floor is sheltered by the high surrounding walls, makes an attractive picnic spot. A litter bin was provided, but in spite of this, people had scattered paper and tins on the grass. I decided to pay homage to the place by picking up the litter and putting it in the bin, and I was pleased when shortly afterwards a young man came in with his dog and proceeded to help me.

From the fort I descended towards Lough Swilly, passing the new Roman Catholic Church at Burt, which is built of stone in a circular design to harmonise with the ancient fort above it. Just below the church I took the road to Burnfoot. This road runs down towards Lough Swilly, and then turns right through a tract of large, level fields. Not long ago this area was a huge tract of marshland or 'slobland', but it has been drained and reclaimed, and it is now excellent farmland. At Burnfoot I joined the main road from Derry to Buncrana, but I soon left it again and took a lane to the right, just past the post office. This lane went uphill over a low shoulder of the range of hills that is dominated by Scalp Mountain. A linkage of small deserted lanes brought me to Fahan, where I joined the main road again, though not for long. I turned down to the shore of Lough Swilly as soon as I could. Here I followed the old railway line for a time, where trains once ran from Derry to Buncrana and beyond. There used to be a connection by ferry across the Swilly to Rathmullan, but now the old pier is crumbling away, and the railway station has become the Railway Tavern.

When the tide is out it is possible to walk on the shore nearly all the way to Buncrana, most of it being good firm sand. But today the tide was in, so I followed the edge of the North West golf course for a time, and then joined the road again to Buncrana. This was the end of my first day's walk, and I returned to Derry by bus.

Day 2   Monday 7 June: to Clonmany

Picking up the trail at Buncrana where I had left it last night, I went down to the mouth of the river Crana, just below the town. Here there is an ancient stone bridge and on the other side a venerable historic building, O'Doherty's Keep. I turned left round this castle and followed a path to the sea. Along this part of the Swilly shoreline there is a well-made path running as far as the beach at Linsfort. This path passes Ned's Point Fort, one of the several forts built to defend Lough Swilly during the years when French forces under Napoleon were threatening an invasion of Ireland and England.

This path is a delightful one for walkers. Mostly raised above the water's edge, it affords open views across the Swilly to the hills of Fanad, and up the broad waters of the Lough to Dunree Head, where the passage narrows again, and then beyond to the open Atlantic. About half a mile past Ned's Point there is a grave beside the path. The inscription on it reads: 'This plaque marks the site of the martyrdom of Friar Hegarty in 1711'. The grave in this lonely spot recalls the days of the harsh Penal laws, when only a limited number of Catholic priests were registered and recognised. Others, who served mass secretly in remote places, were harried and persecuted.

Before long my path descended to Linsfort strand, a large, open stretch of beach, with good firm sand to walk on. After this beach it becomes difficult to follow the coast. There is no regular path, and there are fields and fences running down to the edge of the cliffs. So I turned inland up a lane to join the road to Dunree near Linsfort post office. There was little traffic on this road, but before long I overtook a woman pushing a child in a push-cart. We fell into conversation. She turned out to be an Englishwoman from London, now living in Inishowen. For a time she had been a nurse in the Florence Nightingale Hospital in Johannesburg. When, long ago, I was living and working in Johannesburg, I went to this hospital for a small operation. Was this just a freak coincidence, or is it really a 'small world'?

Passing through a small straggle of houses at Muineagh, I went down towards Dunree beach, or Crummie's Bay, as this inlet of the sea is called. I skirted the bay to the east and crossed a small river, the Owenerk, to reach the slope of the Urris Hills, rising up from the bay. These heathery hills offer delightful mountain walking, with fine views over the sea to the north, and to the south and the west, over all the other hills of Donegal. I selected a good viewpoint and sat in the sun to eat my lunch, looking down at the sea below me.

Soon I dropped down from the ridge and passing two small loughs high up in the hills, Lough Fad and Cranlough, I took a sloping diagonal line down towards Lenan Bay, following an old turf track at the lower end of my route. The day was warm and the sea inviting, so I took a quick swim on Lenan beach, a fine broad strand, facing west, sheltered at both ends by rocky cliffs.

This remote part of Inishowen, cut off by the Urris Hills, was once known as 'the Poteen Republic'. In 1811 the parish of Urris was ordered to pay a heavy fine for making poteen (illicitly distilled whiskey). This was resented by the local men, some of whom equipped themselves with a cannon taken from a wrecked ship, the *Saldahna,* and they ambushed a British force, sent to enforce the law, in the Mamore Gap. Urris remained independent until 1815, when it was finally subdued after another skirmish.

After my swim I continued to follow the coast until I came to my night's lodging at Crossconnel, near Clonmany. In this area there are still some beautifully thatched cottages, thatched in the Donegal style,

159

with the edges tied down against the force of Atlantic gales; but the thatch is inevitably giving way to the modern slate or tiled roof, which is so much easier to maintain.

Day 3   Tuesday 8 June: to Malin Head

A clear blue sky gave promise of a warm summer day, so I put on my shorts. I found a bridge over the Clonmany river, and walked up past a deserted clachan, a small group of farm cottages quietly mouldering away, on to the shoulder of Binnion hill and over the other side, down to the long leisurely curve of Pollan Bay. There was a car park at the edge of the bay, and I noticed a Dormobile caravan parked there. I was having trouble with my watch, so I approached the occupants to enquire what time it was. Mr and Mrs Pollock were from Portstewart, and we had a friendly chat. They were touring in Inishowen, and Mrs Pollock had been puzzled by the signs saying 'Inis Eoghan 100'. She thought it might be the number and name of a house. I was able to explain that it was simply a 100 mile scenic route round Inishowen.

The long curving strand of Pollan Bay was quite empty of holiday-makers. There was just a gently washing sea caressing the sand, and further out the rocky shape of Glashedy island. At one time local farmers used to take sheep out to this island for summer grazing, but now it seems totally abandoned to the sea-birds. In the 1960s, when I first joined the North West Mountain Club, then based in Derry, the club made two attempts to visit Glashedy. Arrangements were made with a local boatman on Doagh island, but when a small group turned up one summer evening the boatman was found to be drunk and not capable of handling the boat. Another visit was arranged, and this time we got into the boat and set off, but we had hardly gone a hundred yards before the boat sprang a leak, and we had to return to shore. So I have not yet set foot on Glashedy.

I was now approaching the end of the bay and coming to the ruined O'Doherty castle at Carrick-abraghy. This is on the furthest reach of Doagh island, which is now no longer an island, but joined to the mainland by a flat strip of sandy soil. There seems to have been a castle at Carrickabraghy since the ninth century. It must have been built and rebuilt many times. What is left of it now is sadly crumbling.

From the castle a road runs round Doagh, following the coast and eventually joining the road from Ballyliffen to Carndonagh. Instead of taking this road, I cut across the centre of Doagh, walking over sand-dunes that were carpeted with wild flowers. There were many orchises, varying in colour from pale mauve to deep purple. There were also buttercups, yellow vetches, and in the damper hollows, yellow irises. There were numerous rabbit burrows in the soft dunes, and overhead the larks were singing.

My plan was to follow the coast as much as I could, but there is no way of getting across the long inlet of Trawbreaga Bay to reach Malin on the other side, except by taking the road and turning inland, through, or near, Carndonagh. I decided to hitch a lift at this point, if I could, to get back to the coastline on the Malin side of the bay. When I had crossed Doagh and reached the road to Carndonagh I began thumbing lifts. I walked some two miles, and about ten cars passed me, but none of them stopped. Then I was picked up by an elderly couple from Dublin, who were holidaying in Inishowen. They took me through Carndonagh and along the Malin Road to the turn-off for Culdaff. I walked on towards Malin, but almost at once a local farmer stopped and offered me a lift. He had worked in England for a time, but now had come home to farm in Inishowen. 'All they think of over there', he said to me, 'is making money'. He dropped me in Malin and I continued my journey along the road to Malin Head, following the coastline once more.

I knew that there had been a Friar's Cell somewhere in this area, so I knocked at a door to make enquiries of its whereabouts. The door was at Rose Cottage, an attractive local thatched cottage, but the girl who came to the door was from Blackpool. She pointed out to me the direction of the Friar's Cell. I walked that way and came to a rocky outcrop. Below it was a rock-shelter. Had that been the Friar's Cell? There was no sign to mark it, so I turned back to the road.

I had only been walking for about ten minutes when a local bus stopped and offered me a lift. This is the first and only time in my life that I have been offered a lift by a bus, without charge, so I gratefully accepted and went as far as Lagg. Here I turned down to the beach at Five Fingers Strand and had another swim. Then I buckled on my rucksack and tackled the stiff climb up the cliffs to Knockmany Bens above. I walked over the rough heathery bens and down to Ballygorman, where I spent the night at Mrs Boyle's comfortable Guest House, *Baraicin,* near Malin Head.

Day 4   Wednesday 9 June:
to Glengad Head

For a time this morning I followed the road that loops round Malin Head, but at the northern end of the loop I left the road to seek the cliffs. I passed the Devil's Bridge, a bridge of rugged rock over a small inlet of the sea. A little further on, moving eastwards now, I sat at the top of a steep cliff, looking down at the sea below and listening to the cries and calls of hundreds of sea-birds. They must have been nesting on the rockstacks below. I could see gulls, fulmars, cormorants, guillemots, and, I think, puffins. The birds were too distant to be identified easily, but the air was loud with their cries.

I went on along the rocky coast, passing the ruined lookout tower. I went below it for a few minutes to stand on the northernmost tip of Ireland. Then I moved back to the road again, and passed the Meteorological Office and the small harbour. I kept to the shore until I passed the 'Wee House of Malin', a small cave where a hermit once lived. Here I turned inland a little to walk over the heathery slopes above Stookarudden, a prominent rock-stack, standing in the sea. Soon I reached Carrickavoel, the Chimney Rock. Here I paused for lunch and sat for a time watching the marvellous pools of translucent green water in the sea far below me. The hill-slopes down to the sea, though steep, were grazed by sheep, which made them like green dropping lawns. Delicate veils of sea-mist drifted up past me, and below was an arch of rock haunted by sea birds. Away beyond, looking silent, remote and unattainable, was the little low island of Inishtrahull.

I was reluctant to leave, but I had to reach Glengad Head for my night's lodging, so I went on over bog and heather, still following the coast. From time to time I was able to follow a turf track. I finally reached Glengad Head, where a fisherman's wife had kindly agreed to give me a bed for the night. The village, or hamlet, of Glengad was small. There was one shop, no post office, and the nearest bar was a mile and a half away. The chief occupations seemed to be fishing and growing potatoes.

Day 5   Thursday 10 June: to Stroove

The good weather I had enjoyed so far came to an abrupt end in the night with a violent thunderstorm, and I set out this morning under threatening skies. I took the road to Culdaff, but long before I reached it heavy rain began to fall. I looked round for shelter, but nothing offered except a solitary house that appeared to be closed and empty. I thought I might find some shelter in the small porch, so I approached the house. Then I saw a small black dog curled up in the shelter of the house-wall. As I came nearer the dog started barking. I thought the house must be occupied, so I knocked at the door. The dog continued barking but no one came to the door. I took off my rucksack and stood in the porch, which gave some partial shelter. Then I noticed an old car standing near by. It had wheels on, but was raised on blocks. I thought I would get better shelter by sitting in it. The front doors were locked, but the rear door opened. I sat in the back while the rain poured down outside. Suddenly I was aware that the curtain at the window of the house nearest to me was being slowly and cautiously drawn across the window. The mystery of the house deepened. There must have been someone inside. A little later, when the rain eased off, I knocked again at the door, to explain and apologise for my intrusion. But still there was no answer and no movement from within. I walked on, pondering the mystery.

When I reached Culdaff, there was little sign of life. I rang the bell at McGrory's Guest House, but there was no response. Soon after, as I was wondering where I could make a telephone call and get a cup of coffee, a young girl arrived and let me in. It was Corpus Christi Day and she had been to Mass, and so arrived early at her day's work. I was able to make my phone call and drink coffee, and then I walked on over the river and headed for the coast again at Culdaff beach.

After Culdaff beach it was difficult to follow the coastline, but a local man directed me to Redford Bay, and I pushed through undergrowth and scrambled over rocks to reach it. Then I had a similar rough course to Tremone Bay. After this the going was easier. I followed the road to Kinnagoe Bay, where there is a pleasant walk along the beach. Then I scrambled up above the cliffs and continued to follow the coastline from above. There were fine views over the sea, but the Scottish islands of Islay and Jura were not visible today. I found a track, which later became a road, that led me to Inishowen Head. Here there is an old lookout post, and below it the rocky head stretching out into the tossing sea. I went down to look at this rugged head, and then turned down into Stroove, where I had secured a bed for the night.

Day 6   Friday 11 June: to Lough Fad

A soft rain was falling this morning, but in spite of this I decided to visit Port-a-Doris, before heading south along the shoreline of Lough Foyle. Port-a-Doris is a fascinating doorway of rock, leading on to a small pebbly beach. I was glad I had seen it, but I soon turned round and took the road towards Greencastle. I left the road and crossed the golf links to reach the shoreline. I was able to follow it all the way to Greencstle, though it was rough going in places, with long wet grass and sodden bracken. It was a gentle, winding shoreline, wooded in places, with some large houses close to the water's edge, all very different from the wild precipitous cliffs of the northern coastline. I passed close by the ancient ruined castle that gives its name to the village of Greencastle. In its decaying state it was indeed a 'green' castle. From its damp and weatherbeaten old walls weeds and wild flowers grew in rich and colourful profusion.

Near the castle is the small harbour of Greencastle. After this the shoreline path becomes more difficult to follow, until finally I struck the made path, just below Ballybrack Lodge, that leads all the way to Moville. After Moville the shoreline becomes less interesting, and the main road south to Muff and Derry is dull, so I decided to turn inland into the hills. I took a lane that led me past Cooley Cross, a tall, striking early Christian high cross which stood just outside an ancient abandoned churchyard, possessing an unusual 'Skull House'.

I continued to follow the lane uphill towards Crockavishane mountain. It was an attractive lane with thick hedges and a number of old cottages. At one thatched cottage I saw an old man with a scythe, wearing home-made leggings. He looked like Father Time himself. I exchanged a few words with him, and I asked him if he lived alone. He replied 'I'm all on my own, and I'm getting older, but I must make the best of it'. With such a calm acceptance of loneliness and age, I'm sure he will make the best of it.

The lane I was following came to an end at a farm which nestled at the foot of Crockavishane mountain. I climbed up to the top, where I had good views over the peninsula, with Slieve Snaght dominating the mountain panorama. Now I was aiming for Lough Fad, in the hills above Redcastle. I had arranged my night's lodging at a house about a mile below this lough. I found it difficult to take a line across the hills in a south-westerly direction, because there was no ridge to follow. The hills dipped up and down, through much wet bog, and the lanes were all running inland across my path. But eventually I reached Lough Fad, and turned down to join my hosts for the night, an elderly brother and sister, living in a small but comfortable bungalow. The brother, now 80, came to join his widowed sister when his wife died. He had been living in Fleetwood in Lancashire, where he had worked for ICI. He said he missed Fleetwood and his local club, but his sister could still drive a car, and they got out twice a week to local towns to play whist and bingo.

Day 7   Saturday 12 June:
to Tievebane

I decided this morning to abandon the line of hills for a time, and rejoin them at Eskaheen mountain. There were Forestry plantations to contend with, in addition to the other problems. I didn't want to walk along the main road, so I took a short bus ride, and then turned up a lane towards Eskaheen. I was on unfamiliar ground here, so I asked several people for directions. They all directed me *by road* to Grania's Gap. Although I had a stick in my hand and a rucksack on my back, the fact that I wanted to walk over the mountain to reach the Gap, didn't seem to be understood. Finally I chose a lane for myself that lead towards the slopes of Eskaheen. On this lane I met a farmer's wife, so I consulted her. She said at once: 'You are on the wrong road', but when I explained that I meant to walk off this road on to the mountain, she agreed that I could go on. So finally I got on to the slopes of Eskaheen, and climbed up to the top. For a short time I had good views over Lough Foyle, but as I descended towards Grania's Gap, the mist and cloud came down.

I had intended to complete my circular tour by following the Scalp range of hills to Tievebane, between Burnfoot and Fahan, but in view of the weather I now decided to leave Scalp in the clouds, and to take the lane below it leading in the same direction. Although at a much lower level, the lane too provides a pleasant walk, and is almost empty of traffic. At Tievebane I took a bus to my base in Fahan, still pondering on the beauty and variety of this rugged peninsula, and deeply satisfied with my six day walk.

The Carrick Circuit

Day 1   Wednesday 8 July:
Bunglass to Glencolumbkille

I drove to Carrick yesterday, and I stayed overnight in a farm Guest House. I was anxious to make an early start in the morning, so I arranged with my hostess to have breakfast at 7.30. Later, when I went to my room, I found a card on the mantelpiece stating 'Breakfast 9.00 - 10.00'. But I have always found Donegal people very obliging.

The weather forecast was promising, and I was looking forward eagerly to the day's walk. As I have already mentioned, some of my friends and

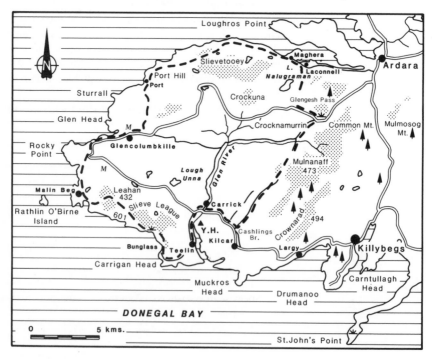

acquaintances have accused me of being 'a glutton for punishment'. I think the word 'glutton' is inappropriate, but I accept the fact that I do sometimes take on assignments that invite punishment. If you go on long-distance walks it is hardly possible to avoid doing so. But I would also maintain that I am a glutton for enjoyment. So far as I can, I take steps to ensure that a walk is enjoyable. So today I packed my towel and bathing costume, and a gourmet picnic lunch. I also made a luxurious flying start, to shorten the distance and reduce the tedium of road walking, by hiring a car to take me to my starting point on the cliffs at Bunglass. The last mile of this road is by no means tedious walking. It is a precipitous mountain road, with fine views over Donegal Bay. But I have walked it several times before, and I was anxious to get on to the cliff footpath.

It was a glorious summer day, with the sun already high up in a blue sky, but there were still a few delicate wreaths of mist curling over the summit of Slieve League, making it seem loftier and more mysterious. Far down below was the blue sea, with the water turning green and white at the edges, where it lapped and licked at the steep rocky shore. I followed the well-worn cliff path, pausing frequently to gaze down from a vantage point at the dizzy, rocky slopes falling to the sea. Slieve League rises to 1,972 feet (about 600 metres) and is the highest marine cliff in Europe. Looking down at the awesome drop below, I was reminded of the famous cliff speech in *King Lear*. Edgar is telling the blinded Gloucester, who wishes to jump to his death, that he is on the edge of a precipitous cliff.

> Stand still! How fearful
> And dizzy 'tis to cast one's eyes so low!
> The crows and choughs that wing the midway air
> Show scarce so gross as beetles .... The murmuring surge
> That on the unnumbered idle pebbles chafes
> Cannot be heard so high. I'll look no more,

169

Lest my brain turn, and the deficient sight
Topple down headlong.

There is no real danger of 'toppling down headlong' from the cliff path, but reasonable caution should be exercised, and the path is best avoided in bad weather. Yet the fearsomeness of the drop adds an edge of excitement to the panoramic views over the coastline.

Slieve League, the highest marine cliff in Europe, rises to 1,972 feet (about 60 metres)

At one point, a little east of the summit, the path climbs over an exposed ridge of rock, known as 'One Man's Pass'. This is not as formidable as it sounds, but I took the precaution of strapping my walking stick on to the back of my rucksack, so that I had both hands free to grip the rock when necessary.

Soon after reaching the summit I saw a group of three people ahead of me. So far I had had the whole mountain and coastline to myself, though there were one or two fishing boats out in the bay. The group turned out to be three young ramblers from Germany. It was their first visit to Ireland, and they were sitting enjoying the view with obvious pleasure.

From the summit I turned inland slightly and descended towards the base of Leahan mountain, which lies between Slieve League and Malinmore. As I climbed over the shoulder of this mountain I found myself looking down on the glittering curve of sandy beach known as the Silver Strand (Trá Bán) at Malinbeg. It was a most beautiful sight, like a glimpse of some tropical paradise. The sun shone down on a clear blue sea (green at the edges) and a smooth curve of golden white sand. I had thought of going over Leahan and direct to Malinmore, but at once I changed my mind and decided that I must go down for a swim on that heavenly beach.

But first it was time for lunch. Although the sun was shining from a clear sky the wind from the west was cool, so I found a sheltering bank, settled down on my old cagoule and unpacked my rucksack. My 'gourmet' lunch consisted of a very small bottle of wine, some salami sausage, blue cheese, bean sprouts, wholemeal bread, cherries and a flask of

171

coffee. Eating on a sunny mountainside is always a pleasure, and I thoroughly enjoyed my picnic. Afterwards I stretched out in the sun and had a short nap.

Then I headed down for the beach, an easy descent over grassy, heathery slopes. I reached the eastern end of the curving strand and walked along, close to the water's edge, until I reached the western end, where the cliffs gave shelter from the cool breeze. Then I enjoyed a delightful swim. The water was cold, but only moderately so, and it was wonderfully clear and clean, so that I found my short swim deeply refreshing. Afterwards I climbed the steps up from the beach to the car park above, and took the road towards Glencolumbkille. I passed by a mixture of holiday houses and small farms. I noticed that grass was still being cut with a scythe and made up into small cocks of hay.

When I reached the Glenbay Hotel at Malinmore I found that I had a considerable thirst. I quenched it with a large pot of tea, lingered, and finally had a meal in the hotel. Then I went on to the Guest House in Glencolumbkille that was my destination for the night. My pedometer told me that I had walked 15 miles, but I was not exhausted, and it had been a wholly enjoyable day. My 'punishment' was yet to come.

Day 2   Thursday 9 July:
to Laconnell

This morning the sky was overcast and a light drizzle was falling, but it was not unpleasant for walking. However, I decided to shorten my planned coastal route a little by going direct to Port. The coastal route, up past the old Martello Tower on Glen Head, and along the edge of the rugged precipitous cliffs past the projecting rock promontory of Sturrall, is much the most exciting way. The cliff scenery is equal to that on Slieve League. But I had been this way only three weeks previously with the North West

Mountain Club, so I went by the shorter inland route, taking a track past the TV mast on the mountain.

This gave me time to visit two of the many interesting archeological sites that abound in Glencolumbkille. The first was a souterrain just outside the door of the Church of Ireland church, which is built on the site of ancient monastic ruins. A covering lid is held down by a big stone. When you lift it up you look down into a stone vault, not unlike a dry well. If you climb down you find two narrow passages leading off in different directions. These are pitch dark, so a torch is essential. I had brought one with me, so I explored both passages. They contain nothing nowadays, but presumably they were used to hide people and valuables in the days of Viking raids. I was glad to emerge again into the open air above. Souterrains are claustrophobic places and I would hate to have to hide in one.

I followed the road across the river, heading for the hills. Soon I passed a local man with a friendly smile. We exchanged a few comments on the weather, which had now improved, and he asked me where I was going. When I told him, he said 'That's a terrible long way. Ah, be God, you have great energy'. I walked on, feeling at least ten years younger. Then I came to a sign that read 'Manornamortee Megalithic Tomb'; I left the road and followed a delightful path between flowering fuchsia hedges and over a well-built stone stile, until I reached the ancient burial ground on the open hillside. There were two Dolmens here, one large and one small. The large one, though not as tall and striking as those at Kilclooney (near Ardara) and Gortnavern (near Carrowkeel), was still very impressive. I was struck, not only by the remarkable technical skill which these Stone Age men must have employed to move such massive boulders, but also by the deep respect that they must have felt for their dead leaders.

I returned to the road and continued my way uphill. Soon I had passed the last cottage and was on the open hillside, following a track that wound up towards the TV mast. Once I had passed the mast, and begun to descend the northern slope of the mountain, the views of the coast began to open before me. I could see the little harbour of Port, and the islands of Toralaydan and Tormore beyond it. A winding green track took me down to Port. As its name implies this was a port or harbour. It is still used by fishing boats, but the fishermen come by car from elsewhere, and the local cottages are deserted. Most of them were in ruins, but one, though uninhabited, was well preserved, and had clearly been taken over as a holiday cottage.

I climbed Port Hill and continued to follow the coastline. Here, too, the cliffs fall precipitously to the sea. One could sit gazing down for hours at the rock-stacks and sea-birds, and the tossing restless sea. But I pressed on because I had a long way to go, and I was not familiar with this route. It proved difficult to follow the coast, because of the many indentations, and the steep slopes of the hills above. I found myself zigzagging up and down, unable to see the coastline ahead of me, until finally I caught glimpses of Loughros Beg Bay.

The evening was wearing on, and I still had to reach Maghera and Laconnell beyond it. I knew that there was a cliff path running above the caves near Maghera. I had been on it some years ago when climbing Slievetooey, but I was not sure where I would find it. However, I did strike it eventually and I did my best to follow it, which was not always easy. At one point I came to a position where it seemed impossible to go on. The path petered out and there was a large slab of wet rock to climb, with meagre handholds. I could see safe ground beyond it, but below was a steep drop. Should I try the climb, or go back? I was reluctant to abandon the path because I thought it would mean my having to take a much longer route over the mountain above it, and I was already late. I debated the matter for a few moments, and then decided to play safe. I retraced my steps and after fifty yards I found to my surprise that I was back on the proper path again. I had gone off on a small diversion, probably made by sheep or goats. I was immensely relieved that I didn't have to go all the way back, and very glad that I hadn't tackled that wet rock. So, in spite of the rain that was now falling again, my spirits rose and I made what speed I could to my Guest House in Laconnell which I reached at 9.00 p.m., sodden but cheerful, and I ate with relish the roast beef that my hostess, who had expected me two hours earlier, had been keeping hot for me in the oven.

Day 3   Friday 10 July: to Carrick

I slept like a log last night and didn't hear the rain beating down, but I awoke to a wet world. The water-fall below Laconnell, that had been a gentle clear stream when I passed it the night before, was now a raging brown torrent. I had intended to climb the green slopes above Laconnell, and make my way through the hills towards Carrick. But my host told me of an old road that I would find further down the village, that would lead me up through the hills in the right direction. So I put on my rain gear and opted for the road. It turned out to be a most attractive 'green' road, probably an old turf route. The surface was hard, but a green band of grass was growing in the middle, and the edges were grassy, too. Even in the rain, I had fine views over the bay below as I climbed up the road. Soon my road joined the river, the same river that becomes a waterfall, pouring over the escarpment in lower Laconnell. It was now in full flood. and I was glad that I had not to cross it.

The road and river followed a narrow pass between mountains, and I did not expect to find any human habitation, but soon a bend in the road brought me in sight of some cottages. I could see smoke coming from a thatched roof and I decided to knock and ask my way, partly as an excuse to get a break from the pouring rain. I was received with warm hospitality and given a seat at once. In the room were an elderly man, a young woman and a toddler in a playpen. At first I thought the latter was a boy, but I soon learnt that her name was Karen Patricia, by a strange coincidence exactly the same names that were given to one of my own granddaughters. The young woman went into the kitchen and soon reappeared with a hot cup of tea and a plate of thin, buttered toast. I was very glad of this, though I could hardly do justice to the tempting toast, because I had already had a large Ulster fry for breakfast. I must have stayed chatting for half-an-hour in the cottage, and I emerged much heartened to face the wet road ahead of me. I had my bearings now, and I had only to follow the roads to reach Crowbane.

At this point on the Ardara-Carrick road I had intended to cut across the hills and follow the Ballaghdoo River to Cashlings Bridge, and so back to Carrick, where my car was waiting. But as I approached Crowbane my immediate preoccupation was to find some shelter for lunch. Anyone who has eaten a picnic lunch in the open, in the rain, will understand why I wanted shelter. I noticed an abandoned cottage, but it had no roof on, and offered very meagre shelter. Then I saw a farmhouse with a large corrugated-iron barn alongside it. I knocked at the farmhouse door and asked if I might take shelter in the barn to eat my lunch. The young farmer readily agreed and turned up a box for me to make a seat. I ate my lunch in good shelter, watched by three farm dogs and about a dozen hens. The dogs were very polite and well behaved, keeping at a respectful distance and only moving when I threw them the odd crust. While I was there I heard a hen cackling as though it had just laid an egg. I looked around me but could not see it anywhere. Then it flew down from an old turf-basket hanging on the wall. I looked in the basket and there were four eggs. I learnt later that hens like to get up high to lay their eggs. Presumably they feel more secure from interruption or interference.

After lunch I looked out at the weather again. It

was still raining steadily and the hills were under cloud. I decided to call it a day and try to phone for a car to Carrick. I had noticed telephone wires going to the farmhouse, but when I asked if I might use their phone, I was told that they were not yet connected to the local exchange. A few moments later the young farmer offered me a lift to Carrick in his own car, which I was very pleased to accept. Later, when he dropped me beside my car, he would take no money, not even towards his petrol. As I drove home in the evening I remembered, not only the magnificent cliff scenery, but the warm friendliness and generous hospitality of the people in south-west Donegal.

Postscript

I don't like leaving a new route unfinished so I returned on a later occasion to explore the last part of the Carrick circuit. At Crowbane (Grid reference G 607804) the road from Ardara to Carrick takes a sharp right turn. A lane leads off to the left, crossing a bridge and passing a farm, heading south towards the hills. After about half a mile the lane turns down to a house and stops. The route lies straight on, across a small stream and up a boggy hillside, keeping well below Mulnanaff mountain, until one reaches a plantation of conifers. Here I followed a firebreak through the plantation until I came to a gate at the end and found a track. This track eventually became a road and led me down to Cashlings Bridge, where it joined the road to Carrick. I followed the road to Carrick and completed my circle.

This inland return from Laconnell to Carrick is less exciting than the coastline, but it offers a way of completing the circuit. Most of the walking is along roads, but the 'green' road up from Laconnell, and the descent from the plantation offer pleasant and interesting walking. Most of the roads followed are free of traffic.

Glenveagh National Park

This fine park, situated in the north-west of Donegal, is now a very popular tourist area. There is a castle to visit, overlooking the long waters of Lough Veagh, and some remarkable gardens, which contain many exotic plants. The setting of the park, which lies along the Derryveagh mountains, is remote and beautiful, and a large herd of red deer roam the hills and woods. There is a visitor centre at the northern end of the lough, which is the official entrance to the park. Here there are many displays and exhibits, and audio-visual shows are available free. Among the exhibits is a large topographical model of the park area, very helpful to anyone planning to walk.

In addition to the general tourist attractions, the

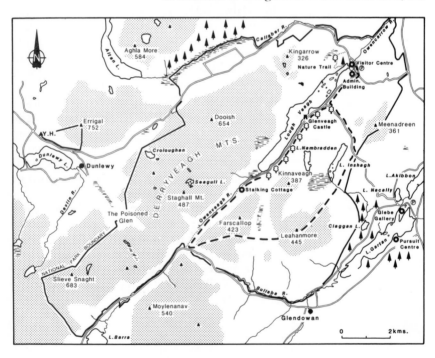

park does offer some fine walks and climbs. The park lands now actually include the two highest peaks in Donegal, Errigal and Slieve Snacht, but these are remote from the central area. It is possible to walk the length of Lough Veagh along a road, tarred as far as the castle, and then gravelled until about half a mile beyond the southern end of the lough. After this it becomes a rough track, following up the glen and the Owenveagh River, until it reaches the Churchill-Doocharry road. On both sides of the glen are wild hills and mountains, with no regular paths or routes.

Cars are not normally permitted past the visitor Centre, where there is ample parking space. When you enter the park and pay the admission fee (adults £1; children, students, OAPs 50p) you will be handed an informative leaflet, which contains an excellent map of the whole park area. The scale of this map is one inch to a mile, or 16 mm to 1 km. This leaflet contains a section on hill walking, which I quote below for the information of intending walkers.

If special permission is sought, consult the superintendent, Glenveagh National Park, Church Hill, Co. Donegal (tel: 074 37088 or 37090).

Most of the park is mountainous and is suitable for properly prepared hikers only. If you intend walking on the hills, please call into the Visitor Centre and leave details of your planned route and expected time of return.

For your own safety:

Do not venture into the hills alone.

Make sure you have proper clothing (including walking boots), maps and compass (and the ability to use them) and sufficient food and spare warm clothes.

Call to the Park Office beforehand if planning a walk on the hills between August and February, when culling of deer may be in progress.

Two of the hill walks within the park are described in *Irish Walk Guides 3* (*see* list of Recommended Reading). One of these is an ascent of Dooish mountain via the Astelleen waterfall, beyond the sandy beach at the southern end of Lough Veagh. The

*Glenveagh Castle,
overlooking Lough Veagh*

During the open season
the minibus may be taken
to this road.

other takes in three modest summits to the east of the glen in the Glendowan mountains. These are Kinnaveagh, Leahanmore and Farscallop (or Scollops). Both these walks present some difficulties, and should not be attempted by inexperienced climbers.

I recently tried out a circular walk, which I will now briefly describe. About half a mile north of the castle there is a gravelled road leading off the tarred road and running south east, through the hills to Gartan Lough. I parked my car near the beginning of this road and then followed it, at first through rhododendron thickets and then over open upland bog country, until I was above Lough Inshagh. Here I paused and looked down at the lough for some minutes. When I turned my head I saw that two deer had been watching me from the crest of the hill behind. I saw many more deer later, when I crossed the hills.

I followed the road almost to the deer fence, then I turned off southwards, heading for Leahanmore. The ground was boggy and somewhat heavy-going. There had been some heavy rain during the days before my walk, but I imagine that the ground is usually soft in this area, because the underlying granite does not absorb water. When I came to the river running out of Lough Inshagh, I found that it was in spate. I had to take off my boots and wade through cautiously.

I climbed up towards the top of Leahanmore. Here I paused for lunch and admired the extensive views. A large part of Donegal was spread out around me. In front rose the dark bulk of Muckish, and beyond it to the north east a good deal of the coast was visible. To the west was the sharp triangle of Errigal, rising above the other hills. To the south there was a broad panorama, including the distant Blue Stack mountains.

I now headed for the shoulder of Scollops. This meant descending to lower ground, some of which was very spongy and rushy. I saw a herd of twelve deer in front of me. They kept their distance, but they did not disappear, and I was able to watch them for quite a long time. I found the marks of deer everywhere, their hoofmarks in the mud, their droppings, and flattened swathes of grass and rushes where they had been lying.

I was glad to descend from the soft slopes of Scollops to the road below. I followed this road, towards Doocharry, for about a mile, and then turned off to the right down a track leading into the Glen. This track brought me to a gate in the deer fence and then down the Glen above the Owenveagh River. I passed the Stalking Cottage and continued down the road alongside the shore of Lough Veagh. This is densely wooded, with tall hedges of rhododendron, a sharp contrast with the bare mountain-sides above. Passing by the Castle, I reached my car again after some seven hours of walking. The distance was about 21 km (13 miles).

This walk gives a good introduction to the park area, and there is a fair chance of seeing deer on the hills, but the going, once off the roads and tracks, is soft and spongy. Good waterproof footwear is essential.

Other Walks in Donegal

The journals and notes above by no means cover all the good walking areas in Donegal. Almost everywhere in the county there are interesting walks to be found. Not far from the Glenveagh National Park there is the Ards Forest Park, on a wooded peninsula stretching out into the sea. Here a number of shorter walks are marked out, with colour guides. Nearby, on the northern coast, are the wild promontories of Horn Head and Melmore Head. Walks round these headlands are described in *Irish Walk Guides 3* (*see* recommended reading list at the end of this book). There are also several attractive islands off the west coast of Donegal, many of which can be reached by boat. Wherever you are in Donegal, if you use your eyes, and your map, you will find good walking.

For further practical advice and information about Co. Donegal, it is worth consulting a Bord Fáilte (Irish Tourist Board) Information Centre. There is one in Londonderry at 40 Foyle Street, tel: (0504) 369501, and another on the outskirts of Letterkenny, just before the main road from Derry crosses the bridge over the Swilly, tel: (074) 21160. It is also worth consulting the Donegal County Council in Lifford, County House, tel: (074) 41066. They may have sketch maps of the Ulster Way.

Maps present something of a problem for walkers in Donegal. There is a half-inch series, available in bookshops. A one-inch series, in Black Outline only, may be obtained from Ordnance Survey Map Stores, Phoenix Park, Dublin 8. It is hoped that the new series of 1:50,000 maps will eventually be completed for Donegal.

Recommended Reading

Robert Lloyd Praeger, *The Way That I Went* (reprinted 1980, Allen Figgis, Dublin, £4.50). Although first published in 1937, this book is still well worth reading, not only for its botanical and geological information (Praeger was a botanist) but for its infectious enthusiasm for the Irish countryside. Praeger called it 'a kind of thank-offering ... for seven decades of robust physical health in which to walk and climb and swim and sail throughout or around the island in which I was born ...' The book ranges over the whole of Ireland, but there is much about the north, where Praeger was born.

E. Estyn Evans, *The Personality of Ireland* (Cambridge University Press, 1973; revised and enlarged edition, Blackstaff Press, Belfast, 1981, £3.95). Professor Evans was formerly Professor of Geography at Queen's University, Belfast. This book studies the interaction of man and his habitat in Ireland and contains much of interest about the Irish landscape.

Ernest Sandford, *Discover Northern Ireland* (Northern Ireland Tourist Board, 1976, revised 1981, £3.50). A useful and informative general guide, with some historical background.

Alistair Rowan, *North West Ulster* (The Buildings of Ireland series), Penguin hardback, 1979, £8.95. A useful guide to all the buildings of note in the counties of Londonderry, Donegal, Fermanagh and Tyrone.

Patrick Simms and Gerard Foley, *Irish Walk Guides 3, North West* (Gill & Macmillan, Dublin, 1979, £1.25). A practical guide, with sketch maps, to hill walks in Donegal and Sligo. A small paperback, meant for the walker's pocket.

Richard Rogers, *Irish Walk Guides 4, North East* (Gill & Macmillan, Dublin, 1981, £1.25). A companion volume to the one above, dealing with hill walks in Ulster.

Joss Lynam (ed.), *Irish Peaks* (Constable, London, 1982, £5.95). Although only part of this book deals with the northern hills, it contains much that is generally helpful.

James Hamill, *North Ulster Walks Guide* (Appletree Press, 1987, £3.95). A useful series of detachable plastic-coated cards, meant for the walker's pocket, describing twenty-two walks in North Ulster, with sketch maps and illustrations.

J.G. Cruikshank and D.N. Wilcock (eds.), *Northern Ireland: Environment and Natural Resources* (Queen's University Belfast, and the New University of Ulster, 1982, £6.95). This is mainly a scientific study. It includes chapters on climate and landscape.